The ABC's of Local Area Networks

The ABC's of Local Area Networks

Michael Dortch

San Francisco · Paris · Düsseldorf · Soest

Acquisitions Editor: Dianne King
Editor: Judy Ziajka
Production Editor: Carolina L. Montilla
Word Processors: Scott Campbell, Deborah Maizels, Chris Mockel
Layout and Chapter Art: Eleanor Ramos
Technical Art: Jeff Giese, Delia Brown
Typesetter: Bob Myren
Indexer: Ted Laux
Cover Designer: Thomas Ingalls + Associates
Cover Photographer: David Bishop

Library of Congress Card Number: 90-70025
ISBN: 0-89588-664-2

Manufactured in the United States of America
10 9 8 7 6 5 4 3 2 1

*A*cknowledgments

In the time-honored tradition of first authors everywhere, I owe apologies and thanks to several people. My apologies to my new-found friends at Sybex, particularly acquisitions editor Dianne King, and Barbara Gordon, Joanne Cuthbertson, and Judy Ziajka, the three editors who neither died nor had me eliminated during any of the several problems and delays I caused while getting this book finished. My heartfelt thanks to them for their support, and to Sybex for asking me to write the book in the first place.

I'd also like to acknowledge the support of some very important people. Thanks to Jerry McDowell of McDowell-Romero Communications for his contributions to my knowlege. Thanks also to David Needle, editor of Bay Area Computer Currents, for providing the forum that attracted Sybex's attention. I also appreciate the hundreds of comments, suggestions, and stories from users, vendors, and consultants that helped develop the view of LANs expressed in this book.

Finally, I'd like to thank Howard Anderson, president and founder of the Yankee Group of Boston, for giving my career as a consultant, analyst, and writer its start. Most important, I thank Helen, my new wife, for all her support and love. This book is dedicated to Howard and Helen, and to all LAN users and managers trying to make some sense of it all.

Contents at a Glance

Chapter 1:	What a LAN is—and Isn't	**1**
2:	The Basic Building Blocks of a LAN	**11**
3:	The Network Operating System	**31**
4:	Network Security	**45**
5:	Using and Maintaining Your Network	**55**
6:	What's Out There: Some Important Network Offerings and Their Vendors	**79**
7:	Do I Need a Network, and If I Do, What Do I Do Now?	**95**
8:	Sharing Resources without LANs—or You May Not Need a Network After All	**111**
9:	Beyond Your LAN: Looking toward the Future	**123**
Appendix A:	Tips for Using the DOS Programs BACKUP and RESTORE	**159**
B:	Industry Guidelines for Virus Prevention and Systems Reliability	**165**
C:	Cabling Issues	**173**
D:	LAN Resources	**189**
E:	Glossary of LAN Terms	**197**

*T*able *of Contents*

Chapter 1: What a LAN Is—and Isn't

LANs: A Basic Definition	2
A Bit of History (and Basic Terminology)	3
So, What Is a LAN?	4
The Features of a LAN	5
What's Wrong with This Picture?	7
In Summary	8

Chapter 2: The Basic Building Blocks of a LAN

It Starts on Your Desk: Terminals, PCs, and Workstations	12
Servers and Printers: The Wealth to Be Shared	15
Network Interface Adapters: Tools for Access	17
Network Cabling: Making the Connections	19
Twisted-Pair Cable	19
Coaxial Cable	20
Fiber-Optic Cable	21
Wireless LANs	22
Topologies: Making the Best Arrangements	23
The Star Topology	23
The Bus Topology	26
The Mesh Topology	28
Tying It All Together	29

Chapter 3: The Network Operating System

What an Operating System Is and Does	32
The Network Operating System: Your LAN's Heart and Soul	33
LAN Access: Protocols and Standards	35
Protocols and Standards in Real Life	36
Media Access Methods: Essential Protocols for LANs	38
Network Management Tools: Your Network's Best Friends	40
Backup Management	41

Power Management   41

Resource Management   42

What's Most Important?   42

Chapter 4: Network Security

What Secure Means   46

Determining What Secure Means to You and Your LAN   47

Securing Workstations and Servers   47

Securing Network Passwords   48

Securing Files and Programs   49

Management-Level Concerns   50

Conclusions   52

Chapter 5: Using and Maintaining Your Network

Your LAN and True Information Sharing   56

Developing Client-Server Computing   58

Your Role in Your Network's Documentation   59

Creating Personal Documentation   59

Creating Task-Specific Documentation   61

Creating Site-Specific Documentation   62

How to Do It   63

Your Role in Your Network's Reliability   65

Backup Files: Your First, Best Protection of Reliability   67

Virus Prevention and You   72

Other Ways You Can Make Your LAN More Reliable   74

Chapter 6: What's Out There: Some Important Network Offerings and Their Vendors

How Basic and Advanced LANs—and the Products that
Support Them—Differ   80

Network Software Differences   81

Hardware Differences   82

Cost Differences   82

Examples of Basic LAN Products   83

LANtastic: A Basic Basic LAN | 84
Invisible Software: Upwardly Mobile Basic LANs | 85
Other Basic LAN Products | 87
The Leading Advanced LAN Products: NetWare, 3+Open, and Vines | 87
NetWare: A Cornerstone in the LAN Marketplace | 88
3+Open: A Software-Hardware Strategy | 89
VINES: A UNIX-Based System | 90
Other Factors in Choosing an Advanced LAN | 90
What Products Tell You about the LAN Marketplace | 91

Chapter 7: Do I Need a Network, and If I Do, What Do I Do Now?

Doing the Right Thing: How to Know That What You're Getting Is What You Need | 96
Assessing Your Needs | 98
Planning Strategically for Effective Solutions | 100
A Final Caution | 102
Decisions, Decisions, Decisions | 102
IBM versus IBM-Compatible PCs | 103
DOS-Based PCs versus Macintosh Computers | 105
Twisted-Pair versus Coaxial Cable | 106
Ethernet versus Token Ring | 107
Making Other Choices | 108

Chapter 8: Sharing Resources without LANs—or You May Not Need a Network After All

Sharing Files, Storage Areas, and Programs | 112
Sharing One Printer—or More | 115
Using Multiuser Systems | 117
To LAN or Not to LAN? | 119

Chapter 9: Beyond Your LAN: Looking toward the Future

Your LAN and New Types of Servers | 124
Today's Servers: Pluses and Minuses | 124

The New Megaservers   125

Communications and Databases: Coming Soon to
Servers on Your Network   127

New Servers + New Services = Client-Server Computing   132

Your LAN and the New PCs   133

PCs and DOS, PS/2s and OS/2: Features and Differences   133

What Does the Macintosh Mean to Your LAN?   137

Advanced Workstations and the Specter of UNIX   140

Your LAN and ISDN   145

Your LAN and Industry Standards   148

Ethernet–Twisted-Pair Transmission Standards   148

Fiber-Optic Transmission Standards   149

Multivendor Network Standards   150

Network Managment Standards   150

Electronic Transmission Standards   151

User Interface Standards   152

Printer Standards   153

A Caveat   153

Your Role in Your Network's Future   153

Joining User Groups   155

Attending Classes and Seminars   155

Reading, Reading, Reading   156

You Make the Difference   157

Appendix A: Tips for Using the DOS Programs BACKUP and RESTORE

Preparing to Use BACKUP   160

Using BACKUP (and RESTORE)   162

Appendix B: Industry Guidelines for Virus Prevention and Systems Reliability

Viruses and System Reliability   166

A Systems Approach to Reliability   168

Appendix C: Cabling Issues

    What Cabling to Use? **175**

    Whose Cabling to Use? **175**

    Where to Put Cabling? **176**

    Who's Responsible for Cabling? **178**

    Some Cabling Details **179**

    How Major Vendors Are Addressing Cabling Issues **181**

    Choices and Costs **185**

    Other Considerations **187**

Appendix D: LAN Resources

    Magazines **190**

    Newsletters, Research Reports, and Seminars **193**

Appendix E: Glossary of LAN Terms

*I*ntroduction

This book is intended to give you a solid, well-rounded foundation of basic knowledge about local area networks, or LANs. Rather than focusing exclusively on a specific LAN product, this book will help you understand the basics of the various types of LANs and the important differences among them and their alternatives.

The main goal of this book is to help you take maximum advantage of the many resources LANs can bring to you and your organization. The focus is not on how LANs work, but on how they can help you work better and smarter.

If you already use a desktop personal computer, or PC, and already use, or are considering using, a LAN, this book is for you. If you're new to LANs, this book will help you become more comfortable and familiar with the basics of computing networks, and their importance to your position and organization.

If you are experienced with LANs and are, or are about to become, a LAN manager, this book is also for you. It can help you learn more about the computing network marketplace and how changes in that market can affect your LAN and the work you do. It also presents specific, valuable suggestions to help you develop "future-proof" networks and strategies for network management and growth.

If you simply want to know more about LANs, you too will find in this book the information you need.

A Guided Tour

Chapter 1 of this book helps you figure out exactly what a LAN is and is not. The chapter gives a bit of history and introduces some basic LAN terminology. Then the main features of most LANs are introduced and compared and contrasted with wide area networks, or WANs. Finally, the ideal LAN is compared with the current reality confronting most LAN users, managers, and vendors.

Chapter 2 defines and describes the basic building blocks of most true LANs, including desktop PCs, interface adapters, and network servers, and how these pieces fit and work together. So-called workstations are compared with more typical PCs. Integration of diverse desktop systems also is discussed.

Chapter 3 describes the features of network operating systems in detail. Differences between basic and more advanced offerings are highlighted, and the chapter offers some guidance in choices that affect your network. Operating systems that support more than one type of PC—for instance, IBM-compatibles and Macintosh computers—are also highlighted.

Chapter 4 focuses on one of the most important features of any network: security. The areas where networks are most vulnerable are discussed, along with the most useful steps users and managers can take to protect their data. The information in this chapter will help you develop unobtrusive preventive measures and incorporate these into day-to-day network interactions.

Chapter 5 discusses procedures to help you use and maintain your LANs. Specific suggestions for improving network documentation and reliability are presented. The goal of this chapter is to provide a complete picture of how working with LANs differs from working with simple PCs.

Chapter 6 presents specific information about what LAN products are available. This section focuses on leading, established offerings and vendors. This section also addresses the strategic and business issues likely to affect these vendors and their future products. This information will help you think about your organization's long-term LAN decisions more clearly.

Chapter 7 asks two questions confronting more users and managers every day: Do I need a network, and if I do, what do I do now? Some concise suggestions, ideas, and considerations are presented to help you come up with the best answer to this question for your specific situation. This section contains information valuable to all readers, whether or not they are already using a LAN or some alternative system.

Chapter 8 presents several economical alternatives to LANs that are appropriate for many situations.

Chapter 9 focuses on important issues that are likely to affect LAN decisions at your organization. These issues range from the growing need for connections among LANs and other networks and computers, to the potential impact of emerging technologies, such as new types of PCs, servers, and operating systems such as UNIX and OS/2. This chapter also disucsses the next generation of LANs, called client-server networks, and the impact of new types of connections, such as the integrated services digital network (ISDN), metropolitan-area networks (MANs), and wide-area network (WANs), on your LAN.

Notice that, although this book attempts to be as generic as possible, in discussions of specific products and other details, IBM PCs and compatibles are emphasized over Macintosh and other computers. This emphasis is intentional, for two reasons. The first is that IBM PCs and compatibles far outnumber other types of desktop computers in today's business networks. The second is that although a Macintosh computer is very different from an IBM PC, the conceptual differences between Macintosh LANs and IBM PC LANs are far less significant than their similarities. Nonetheless, important distinctions between IBM PCs and Macintosh and other computers are noted where appropriate.

This book ends by offering some tips on using BACKUP and RESTORE, two important DOS programs. Some industry recommendations to help protect your computing networks are also included, as is a discussion of network cabling strategies. A glossary of networking terms and a list of vendors, publications, and associations that can help you use and learn more about LANs conclude the book.

*S*ome Final Thoughts

This book is designed to be clear, informative, engaging, and as jargon-free as possible. All important computing terms are defined briefly the first time each appears, as well as in the glossary. Because most business people use IBM, IBM-compatible, or Apple Macintosh computers, items specific to any of these systems are clearly noted.

Perhaps most important to you, discussions of technology take a back seat to discussions of potential benefits, risks, and strategies most important to you and your work. So dive into this book fearlessly. It will help you take maximum advantage of LANs—perhaps the most important and exciting business technology since the PC, or the telephone.

one

1

What a LAN Is—and Isn't

As you have probably discovered already, pinning down just exactly what a LAN is can be difficult. Different people mean different things while using the same terms to discuss LANs. Thus, we will first define *LAN* so we will have a definition upon which we can agree for the rest of this book.

LANs: A Basic Definition

In its most traditional sense, a local area network, or LAN, is a group of desktop computers, located relatively close to one another (or locally) and connected for the purpose of sharing access to computing resources. These resources can range from expensive, high-speed printers to very large hard disk drives, which LANs can treat as central electronic file cabinets for storage of shared files and programs.

However, although this definition is an adequate general description of a LAN's functions, it is an entirely inadequate definition of the term. For example, it does not even hint at the broad range of networks that are now called LANs. Most LANs in businesses today support about five users each, according to market research firms that track such things. Many LANs connect only two computers and a printer.

On the other hand, many LANs connect thousands of devices, spread over thousands of square feet. The United Airlines' "Terminal for Tomorrow" at Chicago's O'Hare Airport has a network that connects more than 30,000 desktop computers, destination signs, and other electronic devices. Nonetheless, the network is a LAN, according to its designers and builders.

How can this be? What do these networks have in common with each other, or with your network?

What most LANs have in common is less a list of functions, and more a list of typical components and methods for doing things. A brief look at LANs from this perspective will reveal more clearly the common elements shared by LANs small and large. It will also help us arrive at a better definition of the term *local area network,* or *LAN*.

A Bit of History (and Basic Terminology)

In the beginning of computing, there was the *mainframe*, a large, powerful central computer. People who wanted to use a mainframe often had to submit requests to computer operators and wait hours or days for their results (assuming they had made no mistakes in their requests, of course).

A bit later, *terminals* were connected to mainframes, so people could submit requests from their desks. A bit later still, *minicomputers* appeared, as did software systems that allowed users to submit requests to central systems *interactively*, instead of in *batches* through a team of operators. Terminals also got "smarter" and were able to support initial processing and editing of requests to central systems, which meant each request tied up the central system for less time.

However, computing didn't really take off until truly *personal computers* appeared in the 1970s or, for business people, until the introduction of the IBM PC in 1981. *Personal computers*, or *PCs*, put on individual desktops processing and storage capacity equivalent to larger systems that were just a few years older.

As PCs proliferated, so did products designed to make PC users more productive. Some of these were too expensive for each PC user to have, yet too beneficial to deny everyone. Primary among these were *hard disk drives*, which offered fast access to large amounts of permanent electronic storage.

One of the first examples of true resource-sharing was the *disk server*, a combination of hardware and software that let a few PC users easily share access to a common hard disk drive. The first disk server, in fact, operated with the *CP/M* operating system, the precursor to *DOS*, the operating system that controls all IBM PCs and compatibles. (Operating systems are discussed in more detail in Chapter 3.)

With early LANs, users shared access to hard disk drives via a computer connected to the drive to be shared, which was designated as the disk server. Software on the connected computer divided the shared hard disk drive into areas called *volumes*, one for each user. Every user's volume looked and acted like one of that user's private disk drives. The hard disk also usually included a public volume that let users share information.

In most of today's LANs, disk servers have been replaced with *file servers*, which are more sophisticated variations on disk servers. Simply put, file servers are better at allowing users to share files with others, and at helping users keep track of their files, than disk servers. Today, some LANs support multiple file servers, each with multiple attached hard disk drives. The most sophisticated LANs support easy network growth, by allowing managers to add servers and drives simply and quickly. (File servers are discussed in more detail in Chapter 2.)

Next to hard disk drives, printers usually represented the device to which most early PC users and managers wanted to share access. Almost every LAN offering now allows shared access to printers. In most cases, the *print server* is actually part of the total LAN software package, and not a separate computer.

With a LAN print server, users may be able to use only the printers attached to certain file servers, or they may be able to use printers attached to any user workstation on the network. The LAN manager may be able to restrict access to certain printers. Users may also be able to send several documents to the same printer, with requests queued (held in a queue, or grouped in the order they're received) and managed by print spooling or print queuing features of the print server. These and other features depend on the features of the LAN software being used.

Other types of servers also are beginning to appear. These include *communications servers* and *database servers*, which are both discussed later in this book. For the moment, you need only know that they represent two more examples of the power and benefits that can be distributed to LAN users.

So a LAN is usually thought of as a collection of desktop PCs connected to computers designated as servers via one or more types of *media*, which are often some type of wiring. However, this is basically the same definition we tried earlier, but with more LAN-specific terminology.

S̲o, What Is a LAN?

To completely describe LANs, two definitions are needed: one functional and one technical. Functionally, a LAN is what it was described as earlier: a group of desktop computers and other systems, located reasonably close to one another, connected in ways that allow their users to communicate and to share computing resources such as printers and storage devices. This definition applies equally to LANs in offices, on factory floors, and in research laboratories. In all types of applications, LANs permit groups of computer users to gain access to and share computing resources.

Technically, a LAN is a network of computers connected by specific types of transmission media (such as cables) and network adapters and overseen by any of a number of network operating systems that support all necessary communications protocols and standards. (Protocols and standards are discussed in Chapter 3.)

The distinction between a technical and a functional definition is very important, especially if you are more interested in available functions and services than in how the technologies involved work.

Too often, those who are more technologically oriented like to concentrate on questions such as which LAN alternatives offer the fastest data transmission rates or support the largest number of communications protocols. These questions can be important, but should be asked only after everyone involved is sure that the system in place or under consideration can support the work users need to do. With LANs, every solution's functional value is always more important than its technical elegance.

A LAN is not just a coordinated set of specific technologies, any more than it is just a network operating system. A LAN, when set up appropriately, is a solution to a problem. The problem is how to allow workers who are already working together and already using desktop computers to do both more efficiently. The solution is a system that allows easy communication, information sharing, and collaboration among all relevant users. This system can be a LAN. (Note, though, that although a LAN is a potential solution, it is by no means the only one. Alternatives are discussed in detail in Chapter 8.)

The Features of a LAN

A LAN is also defined by its features. Features are different from components, which are discussed in detail in the next chapter. Specific components can differ, but most LANs share many of the features delineated in the following paragraphs.

Limited Geographic Scope

A LAN typically spans a single office or workgroup, a few floors in a building, or a few buildings in a campus-like setting. This makes LANs fundamentally different from MANs (metropolitan area networks) and *WANs* (wide area networks), which are designed to span entire cities, countries, or continents. LANs use different *protocols*, or rules for information transmission, than these other types of networks and tend to carry information at transmission rates different from those supported by MANs or WANs.

Relatively Limited Number of Users per LAN

Although some types of LANs can and do support hundreds of users on a single network, most LANs support fewer than five people each. Growth usually happens by linking these smaller LANs, rather than by creating very large single networks. This approach is usually easier to manage than a single large network and limits the destructive effects of network failures.

High Reliability

LANs tend to be highly reliable, even when demand for network access is heavy. LAN system software tends to include many features to protect against, detect, and correct transmission errors. Some LANs also support *redundancy*, or duplicate components such as servers or power supplies. A second server, for example, may store backup copies of everything on the first server and be activated instantly if the first server fails. This backup facility allows the network's users to continue working while the first server is being repaired and reactivated.

Expandability

Most LANs can be changed or expanded easily, although the ease of LAN modification depends as much on the design of the cabling plan as on the features of the particular LAN product. Cabling is discussed in more detail in the next chapter.

Heterogeneity

Most market-leading LANs reflect the nature of desktop computing in today's businesses: multiple manufacturers' products, everywhere. Early LAN products were designed primarily to connect multiple IBM-compatible PCs, but most advanced LANs now support multiple types of desktop systems, operating systems, media, and *topologies*, or methods of physical arrangement of components.

Management and Security Features

Most LANs also include numerous features of specific interest to network managers, such as records of user activities and network problems. Many LANs also support features that promote network security, from simple user passwords to more elaborate schemes to limit access to network resources. (Network security and reliability are discussed extensively in Chapters 4 and 5.)

What's Wrong with This Picture?

As you can see, a LAN that encompasses even some of the preceding features delivers several advantages to its users and managers. These include relatively easy shared access to computing resources, relatively easy communication and collaboration among colleagues, and more productive use of PCs by their users.

However, certain problems keep most LANs from approaching the ideal for their users and organizations. Most LANs are harder to choose, buy, install, use, and manage than anyone believes when the process of considering a LAN begins. This is due partly to inappropriate expectations, fueled by inaccurate or incomplete information about a particular LAN or its potential users.

Many resellers are still figuring out how to sell and support LANs successfully, according to many trade press reports and industry analysts. Just as LANs are used and managed differently from PCs, they require different marketing and support strategies, and not every good reseller of PCs can sell or support LANs with equal success. In addition, many producers of LAN offerings are still figuring out the best ways to select and support resellers.

Also, there are many more LANs than there are sources of well-trained LAN managers or users. Few universities offer degrees or comprehensive courses that are LAN-specific. Seminars offered by vendors can be valuable, but may be too product-specific or expensive for many who might benefit from them.

Even when access to education is available, it must be updated and expanded constantly to keep pace with the tumult that appears to be a constant in the network marketplace. Technologies, products, and *industry standards* (discussed later) continue to appear, evolve, and rise or fall in acceptance. All these factors affect the choices available to managers and the information users need to know.

To avoid being buffeted about repeatedly by the effects of the LAN marketplace, those affected by it must get a hold on it, an understanding of "the big picture" and their role in it. Help with this task is one of the underlying purposes of this book.

*I*n Summary

To sum up, a LAN is many things. To its users, it is consistent access to useful computing resources via familiar desktop computers. To managers, it is the system that provides this access and the tools needed to run it effectively. To its designers, it is a combination of technologies. To its marketers, it is a piece of a larger strategy for success in the marketplace.

Whether you are a user or a manager, you would do well to look at LANs as strategic tools for your own job satisfaction and the success of your work group and organization. This perspective can help you appreciate your LAN, your role in its effectiveness, and its role in your work. It can also help you take maximum advantage of the computing resources available to you. As a first step, we'll look at the specific components that comprise many LANs and how these components fit together.

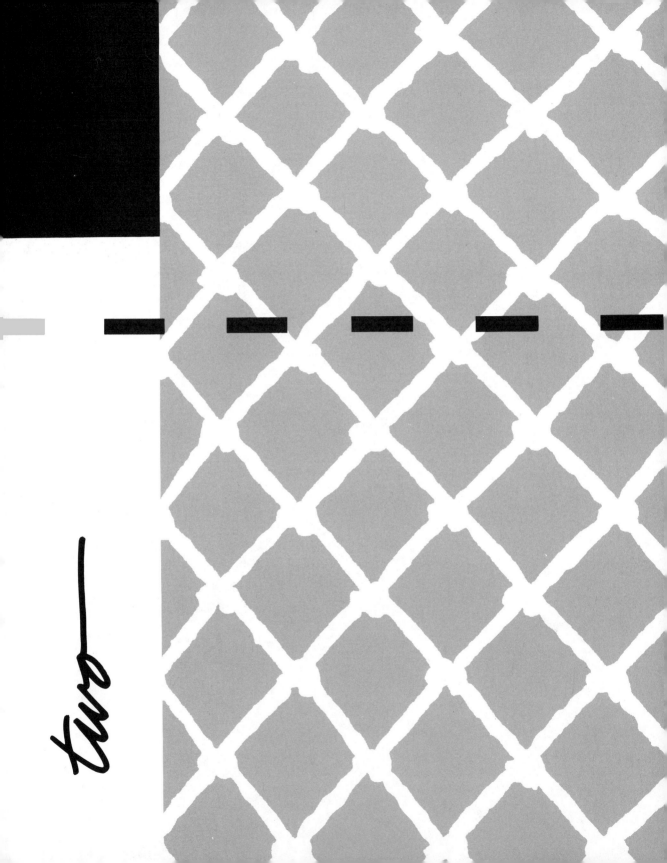

two

The Basic
Building
Blocks of a LAN

A great restaurant needs both talented chefs and a superb service staff. An excellent performance depends equally on a first-rate cast and the best available backstage crew. Your identity is a combination of your body and your personality. In a similar way, LANs are made up of two sets of basic components that work in harmony.

In a LAN, the first of the two sets makes up the physical network and includes all the *hardware*, from computers to cables and connectors. The second set of elements can be thought of as the logical network. The logical network includes what LAN users see on their screens and printers, the services available to users and managers, and the software that contains the instructions that let the hardware act like a network.

As you'll see, various physical and logical items are combined in numerous ways to provide the services, features, and benefits LAN users and managers expect. This chapter and the next take you on a whirlwind tour of the important parts of a typical LAN, beginning with the hardware. This tour will help you see how the various parts of a LAN fit together.

It Starts on Your Desk: Terminals, PCs, and Workstations

To LAN users, the most obvious and important physical components are the computing systems on their desks. These can range widely in power, sophistication, and features. Some may be so-called dumb terminals of the type connected to early mainframes and minicomputers. These terminals are little more than screens and keyboards and depend on connection to some other computer for the power to do anything useful. Although dumb terminals have been in use since computing's earliest days, new technologies continue to make them economical and popular.

Other desktop systems may be PCs or workstations that are powerful computers even before they are connected to a LAN or another system. Unlike dumb terminals, PCs have their own computing power and system memory and the ability to store information on removable *floppy disks* or fixed, high-capacity *hard disks*.

Most of today's desktop PCs are equipped with fast, powerful internal computer chips, large storage capacity (usually via high-capacity hard disk drives), and lots of *random-access memory* (RAM) chips, for system memory. These features allow PC users to perform complex tasks more easily and quickly than was possible with older, less powerful PCs.

The two most popular types of PC in today's offices are very different, even though they are often used for similar tasks. The IBM PC family, originated in 1981, is now the corporate standard throughout the United States. Most desktop PCs are either manufactured by IBM or are designed to be *IBM compatible*. IBM-compatible systems are built with components designed to comply with standards set and made available to other manufacturers by IBM, without violating IBM's patents and copyrights by being exact duplicates of IBM components.

IBM-compatible systems often are less expensive than equivalent systems manufactured by IBM. However, inexpensive clones are sometimes built with components of less consistent quality than that of IBM-chosen parts. Also, many large corporations already have extensive investments in IBM computing systems and choose consistency over discounted prices.

Nonetheless, few IBM-compatible LANs consist exclusively of IBM-manufactured PCs, in part because some compatibles include features that are unavailable or very expensive if purchased from IBM. Compaq Computer Corporation, for example, manufactures IBM-compatible systems that are easily portable and that are sometimes equipped with more features than similar systems from IBM. These features, along with Compaq's focus on high-quality products, has allowed the company to sometimes charge prices higher than IBM's and remain successfully competitive.

The second most popular type of desktop computer is the Macintosh family, produced by Apple Computer Company. When it was introduced in 1984, the original Macintosh computer was dismissed by many as a toy, not fit for serious business applications. However, the system, with its picture-oriented screens and emphasis on simplicity, attracted too many converts for corporate computing managers to ignore. Apple then began improving the Macintosh, and developers of leading business software from the IBM-compatible world began supplying Macintosh versions of their products.

Today, the current crop of Macintosh computers includes sufficient power and memory to run business applications not available even for most IBM-compatible PCs. In addition, Macintosh computers can now be equipped with disk drives that can work with disks from either other Macintosh computers or newer IBM-compatible PCs.

So far, Apple has refused to publish sufficient details about its Macintosh product family to allow manufacture of compatible systems by other companies. However, both Apple and a wide variety of other manufacturers supply enhancements for Macintosh computers, such as video screens that show an entire, full-sized page of text at a time. Some of these enhancements allow easy connection of Macintosh computers to LANs designed primarily to support users of IBM-compatible PCs, as you'll see later in this chapter.

Desktop PCs are now routinely equipped with hard drives that can hold 50 to 70 million *bytes* (specifically sized segments) of information, compared with the 360 thousand to 1.4 million bytes most floppy disks can hold, depending on their type and age. Single desktop systems equipped with 16 million bytes of chip-based system memory also are becoming more common. (A typical single-spaced typewritten page usually uses about 2,500 bytes.)

These large storage capacities, along with faster processing speeds, make today's desktop PCs incredibly flexible and powerful, comparable to systems that filled closets or rooms a few years ago. Needless to say, sharing such power seems like a good idea and is something LANs can help make possible in a variety of ways.

Another type of desktop system combines some of the features of terminals and PCs. The *diskless workstation* is designed specifically for use on LANs and other networks. Like a terminal, a diskless system has a keyboard and a screen, along with a built-in connector for use on a network. Like a PC, it usually contains some system memory. It may also contain information on chips that allows its user to connect to a LAN without loading initial information from a floppy disk, a task often necessary with PCs on LANs.

Although less expensive and simpler than a full-fledged PC, a sophisticated diskless workstation can be used to perform many of the same tasks as a PC on a LAN. In addition, some diskless workstations can be upgraded to PCs with the addition of floppy disk drives, hard disk drives, and other components. A basic diskless workstation, equipped to boot, or start, network software without a floppy disk drive, can cost as little as $250, depending on the features and quantity purchased.

Desktop systems more powerful than typical PCs also are becoming more common among users of business LANs. These too are often called workstations. These workstations are usually designed for connection via networks and are almost always faster, more powerful, and equipped with bigger and better screen displays than conventional PCs. You can read more about advanced workstations and their potential effects on your organization's LANs in Chapter 9 of this book.

Servers and Printers: The Wealth to Be Shared

If you already use a desktop PC, it likely has a hard disk drive of its own, where you keep most of your files and the programs you use every day for applications such as word processing and spreadsheet preparation. With a LAN, most users continue to keep copies of their own files and some programs on the hard drive of their own PCs.

However, LANs are for sharing resources, and files and programs are resources. If you work as part of a group, you are probably already sharing access to paper files, reference works, and the like with your colleagues. This is far more efficient and economical than giving every worker his or her own complete set of files and references and keeping all those sets current.

Similarly, LANs help PC users share access to files and programs, by storing master copies of these in a central location, managing each user's access, and keeping track of modifications to shared files. LAN users can also share access to printers, especially expensive laser printers and plotters that draw detailed diagrams.

The first LANs were designed, in fact, to allow sharing of hard disk drives and printers, because these devices were too expensive to distribute to every user. Today, LANs allow users of PCs both with and without hard disks equal access to these valuable resources.

As you read in Chapter 1, disk servers originally helped groups of PC users share access to hard disk drives and have now largely been replaced by file servers. With file servers, users don't have to know which volume contains a desired file, a necessity with disk servers. The user simply requests the desired file, and the file server's software finds and delivers it. File servers also offer varying levels of security to protect your private information from unauthorized eyes.

. Servers can all be located in the same place, for ease of management and repair, or distributed to various locations on the network. In LANs with multiple servers, the network software you're using determines whether or not you need to know the name of the server that holds the file you want (as is discussed later in this book).

Although most office networks require the capacity of only a single server, some have multiple servers anyway. A second server can store backup copies of all data on the primary server and be activated instantly should the primary server fail. This system allows network users to continue working while the first server is being repaired and reactivated.

Servers can be *dedicated* or *nondedicated*. A dedicated server is used only as a server, whereas a nondedicated server can also be employed as a user's workstation. Whether you can choose the type of server in your LAN depends on the network software your organization uses, as discussed in Chapter 3.

With nondedicated file servers, fewer PCs are required for servers and workstations, and the network may be less expensive than one that uses dedicated servers. However, unless the fastest, most powerful, and most expensive PCs are used as nondedicated servers, overall network operations will likely be slower than they would be if dedicated servers were used.

Also, if someone using a nondedicated server as a workstation experiences a problem with an application, that problem could disrupt the work of everyone else on the network connected to that server. For example, if an application causes a server-workstation to stop operating unexpectedly and the server-workstation must be restarted, every network operation underway at that time may need to be restarted as well, even though no other network users are having problems of their own.

Most users and consultants agree that dedicated servers are the better, safer choice in almost all cases. In fact, some LAN managers unplug and remove the keyboards of the PCs being used as servers and connect them only when a server needs service.

As the computers used as servers become more powerful, they can perform more diverse tasks. They can function as print servers or *communications servers* (that manage access to communications facilities such as modems, discussed later in this chapter) or *database servers* (that manage access to shared stores of information). Powerful servers, along with desktop systems, literally "make" most true LANs. Chapter 9 provides additional information about the evolution of network servers.

Network Interface Adapters: Tools for Access

Desktop systems, servers and other components all must have physical access to some type of network pipeline. Most IBM and compatible PCs use *network interface adapters*, also referred to as network interface cards (or NICs), LAN cards, or network cards.

Network interface cards share some feature in common with *modems* (or modulator/demodulators). A modem lets a PC talk on the telephone to another PC, to a larger computer, or to a computing network. Many people use PCs and modems to access networks to which they subscribe, such as The Source, CompuServe, or MCI Mail. Such networks provide a variety of services and entertainment, from electronic mail to airline reservations to interactive games.

Sometimes, a PC's modem is internal and consists of a board of chips and circuits that plugs into an expansion slot inside that PC, like a network interface card. Sometimes, the modem is a separate small box that plugs into a *serial communications port* (or outlet) on the PC. That serial port can be built in, or it can be on a card plugged into an expansion slot. In all cases, the modem performs the same tasks via a telephone line that a network interface adapter does in a LAN. It gives that PC's user access to the power of a computing network.

Like an internal modem, a network interface adapter plugs into a PC's expansion slot and provides a connector into which a network cable can be plugged. The network interface adapter usually also contains processors that translate signals as they pass between the network and the connected device. Just as with interface cards that connect printers, display screens, and other devices, the specifics of the network interface adapter depend on the type of network and desktop computer to be connected. Figure 2.1 shows the placement of network interface adapters and other components inside a PC.

All Macintosh computers, unlike most IBM-compatible PCs, come already equipped to participate in networks based on AppleTalk, Apple Computer's own network scheme. Instead of extra network interface cards, most Macintosh computers can be connected to a network via their printer ports, which also act as what Apple calls LocalTalk connectors.

However, this Apple-designed network scheme, the components of which are called AppleTalk and LocalTalk, is slow and limited in function compared to many network schemes used by IBM-compatible systems. To be full participants in networks made up primarily of IBM-compatible systems, Macintosh computers need help.

When an expansion slot is available, the Macintosh can be equipped with a network interface adapter, just like an IBM-compatible PC.

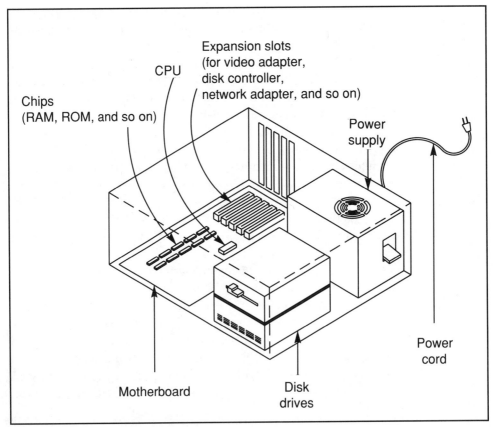

Figure 2.1: *Inside your PC's system unit.*

Adapters that plug into the Macintosh disk drive port also are available, as are devices that act as bridges from Macintosh-based networks to networks designed primarily for IBM PCs and compatibles.

Network interface adapters range in cost from about $100 to $300 or more. The price depends on the adapter's features and manufacturer and whether you buy it from a visiting salesperson, from a retail outlet, or by telephone, mail, or FAX from a discount distributor. In mid-1989, both Novell and 3Com began lowering prices on network interface adapters and other hardware, a promising step toward more affordable LANs.

Network Cabling: Making the Connections

When all your desktop computers, printers, and other devices are equipped with their network interfaces, they need something to connect their connectors. That something is usually some type of cable or wire.

A little knowledge of LAN cabling can be very helpful to you and valuable to your organization. Many LAN managers find that the majority of hardware problems their users report involve cabling or connections to it. Also, the total cost of cabling and connectors for each workstation, and workstation installation, can exceed the cost of the workstation itself. Cabling is one of those network issues that isn't glamorous, but is very important.

The two most popular types of LAN cable are *twisted-pair* and *coaxial*, or coax (pronounced *co-ax*, not *quacks*). In addition, some networks use fiber-optic cable.

Twisted-Pair Cable

Twisted-pair cable is made up of pairs of copper wire twisted together in precisely calculated fashions, because the wires carry more information further when so twisted together than when left as separate strands. For LANs, two varieties of twisted-pair cable are used: shielded and unshielded. Shielded twisted-pair cable (shown in Figure 2.2) is more thoroughly insulated, or shielded, from electrical interference than unshielded cable. This makes shielded twisted-pair cable more reliable

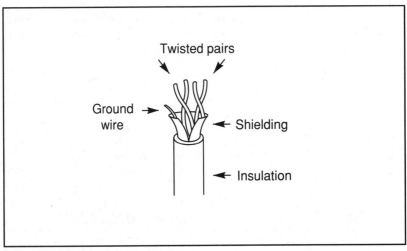

Figure 2.2: Shielded twisted-pair cable.

(and more expensive) than unshielded twisted-pair cable. Nonetheless, unshielded twisted-pair cable is widely and successfully used throughout the LAN marketplace.

Some organizations have been able to use existing telephone wiring, which is usually unshielded twisted-pair cable, for their LANs. This requires, among other things, extensive testing of the wiring to make sure it is reliable enough to carry computer information. To use existing wiring successfully, you also need a detailed map of where the existing cable goes, so problems can be tracked down easily and quickly. If you experience frequent problems with your LAN for no apparent reason, it may be time for extensive testing of your LAN wiring.

Coaxial Cable

Coaxial cable contains a single central wire, which is surrounded by special insulation and wire mesh. Coaxial cable for LANs is the same type of wire that delivers your cable television signals.

There are many types of coaxial cable, all of which can carry more information farther and faster than shielded or unshielded twisted-pair cable. However, coax is more expensive to buy, install, and maintain, and often is harder to work with, than either type of twisted-pair cable. Even so, because coax can carry more information and is available in fire-resistant and water-resistant varieties, coax is the medium of choice for many LAN builders and vendors. Figure 2.3 shows a typical coaxial cable.

Fiber-Optic Cable

The least common type of network cable is the one that may have the most impact on LANs in the future: *fiber-optic* cable, which contains a hair-thin strand of *optical fiber* surrounded by special shielding and insulation. Optical fibers carry pulses of light, instead of bursts of electricity. With the right supporting hardware (that speaks with light instead of electricity), fiber-optic cable can carry more information further in less space than any other type of cable.

Fiber-optic cable is also almost immune to electrical interference and emits no electrical signals that can be tapped from a distance—a feature neither twisted-pair nor coaxial cable can claim. However, fiber-optic cable is the most expensive of the three types to purchase and install. In addition, because one fiber-optic cable may be carrying as much information as hundreds of twisted pairs of copper wire, a break in a fiber-optic cable could affect many more users than a break in another type of cable.

So far, only telephone companies and organizations with very extensive networks have made the jump to optical fiber. Also, industry standards

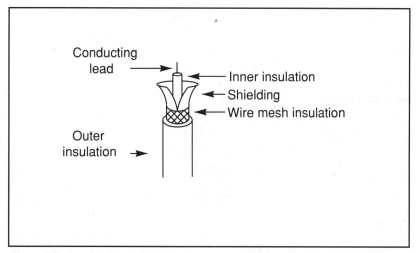

Figure 2.3: *A typical coaxial cable.*

for the way LANs are built with fiber-optic cable are still evolving (as are the standards for some LANs built with twisted-pair cable). However, its use is increasing, and it is becoming less expensive. For a building where LANs on multiple floors are connected, or on a LAN where security is very important, fiber-optic cable may be the right choice for at least part of your network cabling.

Figure 2.4 illustrates fiber-optic cable.

Wireless LANs

Several types of wireless LAN products are also emerging. Some of these are based on radio technology, and others use infrared light, which is invisible to humans under usual working conditions. This type of solution is ideal for interim additions and changes to a larger, cabled LAN. It can also be used to create an easily-activated backup LAN when problems plague a cabled LAN. In addition, wireless technology can be a benefit to a workgroup that wants to experiment with LANs

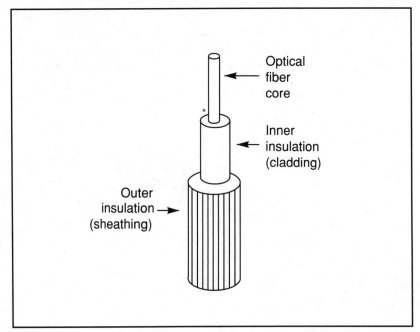

Figure 2.4: *A typical fiber-optic cable.*

before making a serious, long-term commitment. For the predictable future, though, most LANs will be wired, with twisted-pair, coax, or fiber-optic cable.

*T*opologies: Making the Best Arrangements

As you can probably imagine, all the various devices and cable in a LAN can be connected in dozens of different ways. However, only a few of them work well enough for actual LANs. Because your LAN's *topology*, or physical layout, can affect the way your LAN works and how you solve problems on your LAN, you should know something about network topologies.

If a network is very small and simple, it can be composed of straightforward, direct connections between all involved devices. These are called *point-to-point* connections and are simple and sufficient, provided only a small number of devices are connected and users supported.

However, most LANs use the *star*, the *ring*, or the *bus* topology, or architecture. If your LAN is older than one year, or is new but relatively small, it is most likely based on the bus or star topology. If your LAN is new and is large or likely to grow, it may be a ring-shaped network, since the token-ring LAN is growing rapidly in popularity.

*T*he Star Topology

The star is the oldest and most familiar network topology, although you may not realize how familiar. It is the topology upon which our everyday companion, the telephone network, is built.

The home telephone system uses a central switching office to which every home is connected by lines that radiate out from the central office in the shape of a star. Central offices also are linked together, so you can call someone in an area outside the one served by your local office.

Many businesses own a telephone switching system, called a *PBX* (or private branch exchange) that performs the same function as the central office, but for a building instead of a neighborhood. The PBX is the business's direct connection to the local central office.

In a similar fashion, star-shaped LANs have a central computer from which a line is run to each connected workstation and device. Every communication from every user's workstation goes through the central computer before reaching its destination. This makes the central computer (which also acts as the file server and print server) also the focus of network management, including troubleshooting, security, and periodic maintenance.

As with the telephone network, links among central computers allow users to communicate and work together, even if they're not connected to the same central computer. If the star topology has a serious drawback, it is the fact that the failure of a central computer can knock every directly connected user off the network as well. In a large network made up of numerous connected central computers, the failure of one central computer could disrupt communications across most or all of the network.

Sometimes, star-shaped LANs are built with duplicate (or redundant) central computers. This allows rapid recovery from failure of these key network components, although redundancy is a slightly more costly approach.

Figure 2.5 illustrates the star topology.

The ring topology eliminates a LAN's dependence on a central computer by distributing some of that central system's responsibilities to all the other connected workstations. In a ring, each workstation is connected to its neighbor on either side, with the whole network forming a ring, or circle.

Every workstation on a ring network has a unique software address. When a user wants to, say, send a memo or file to another user electronically, the network software automatically puts that note in an electronic envelope that has the addresses of the sending and destination workstations. Whenever a message arrives at the network, each workstation it passes compares the message's destination address with its own address. The workstation then keeps the message or passes it on, as required to get it to its ultimate destination.

When a message reaches its target, that workstation sends a copy of the message it received back to the sender. This return message allows errors to be detected and corrected without the intervention of a central computer. Although ring networks can be constructed that allow messages to travel in either direction around the ring, information almost always travels in only one direction at a time.

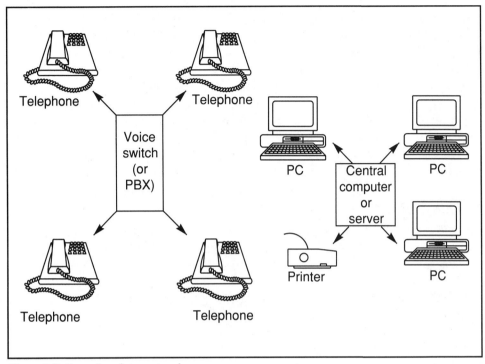

Figure 2.5: *Examples of star networks.*

Every workstation on a ring network listens to see if the network is clear before sending a message. This helps avoid collisions between messages, which would require that everybody try sending their messages all over again.

Network software uses various methods to decide which workstation is allowed to transmit at any particular time. In the most popular method, the software passes a token from workstation to workstation, with only the workstation with the token allowed to transmit. (This method is the foundation of the token-ring LAN software discussed later in this book.) Software for ring networks also must contain tools to guard against messages with bad addresses, which can circle a ring forever, or destruction of the software token.

Information travels around a LAN as electrical impulses, which may lose energy as they travel. Network interface adapaters for ring networks therefore include *signal repeaters*, electrical devices that boost these impulses along their journeys. Some interface adapters for workstations in ring networks also include special circuits that disconnect the adapter from the ring when that adapter's workstation fails. This allows the rest of the users on the network to continue working while the failed workstation is being repaired or replaced.

These circuits also allow managers to add users to a ring network without shutting down current users. However, the best ring networks involve few users, separated by short distances. Users can experience considerable declines in speed and performance when ring networks grow.

Figure 2.6 illustrates the ring topology.

The Bus Topology

The *bus* topology is the only one of the "top three" topologies with a name not descriptive of its shape. In bus networks, all the workstations are attached to the same bus, or cable, with a file server (or a device

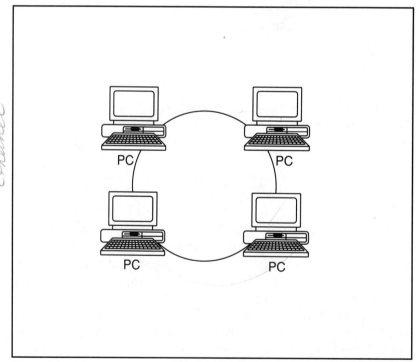

Figure 2.6: *A ring network.*

called a bus controller) at one end. Users' information and requests for files "ride the bus" to and from the "bus terminal" (the server or controller) to get to their destinations.

As with ring networks, every device on a bus network has a unique address. Bus networks can be managed and controlled centrally, like stars, or in a distributed fashion, as is often the case with rings. Central control and management software can reside in the file server or controller at the end of the bus or within a designated *node* (a workstation or other computer) on the network. Distributed management and control work much the same as they do in ring networks.

The bus topology is one of the most popular in today's LAN marketplace. One reason for this popularity is that its wiring requirements are comparatively simple, and growth is accomplished easily and quickly. Also, with most bus-structured networks, workstations can fail or be added without disrupting the rest of the network.

Devices on bus networks can't be too close together, or they will cause electrical interference that disrupts accurate communications. Bus-structured networks that grow can also require additional amplifiers and similar devices to help signals complete their journeys, as with ring networks.

Figure 2.7 illustrates the bus topology.

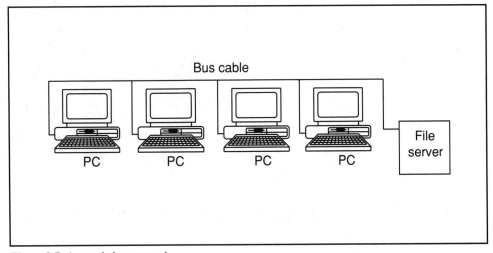

Figure 2.7: A sample bus network.

The Mesh Topology

One other topology is used primarily in networks that are not LANs. It's called a *mesh* topology and is made up of multiple point-to-point connections. Mesh networks can get very complicated very quickly, because many connections must be managed in a network of any size. In addition, reliability requires redundancy, or multiple backup versions of key components, which mean even more connections and chances for problems.

For most LANs, whatever benefits the mesh topology might offer are far outweighed by the additional complexity and management requirements. Also, the extensive cabling requirements can make mesh networks far more expensive to buy and install than networks based on other topologies. Nonetheless, some LANs may grow into mesh networks. Also, a larger network with which your LAN may communicate may use the mesh topology. Figure 2.8 shows a mesh network.

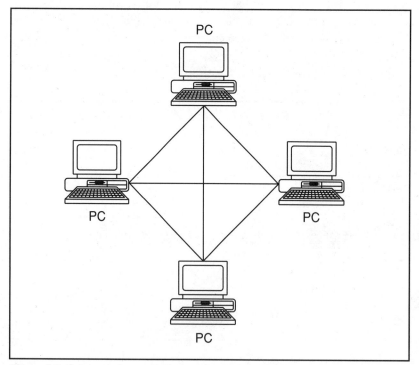

Figure 2.8: *Point-to-point connections and a mesh network.*

*T*ying It All Together

A LAN's basic building blocks are its desktop computers, servers, printers, and disk drives, and the interfaces, cables, and connectors that link everything together. Other physical components can be added, but this list includes all the basics for most LANs.

It is virtually impossible to construct a LAN with physical components all made by a single manufacturer, though sometimes all the physical components can be purchased through a single reseller. Most often, though, the typical LAN requires negotiations and relationships with several separate vendors and offerings from multiple manufacturers.

This presents a potentially problem-filled situation for users and managers. Managers must pick and choose carefully among a bewildering list of offerings and sources. Users must become familiar with all the relevant offerings to get the most from their LANs and to solve problems quickly.

Fortunately, the leading vendors of LAN software constantly update and expand the types of hardware they support. In addition, hardware and software manufacturers attempt to conform to widely accepted standards, established by leading vendors and independent coalitions of vendors, users, and regulators known as *standards bodies* and discussed in more detail in Chapter 3 and elsewhere.

However, the primary responsibility for making sure your hardware works together rests with you who buy and use it. Assurances from vendors should be backed up with written guarantees and proof before purchase whenever possible, to ensure that the building blocks of your LAN form a firm foundation.

three

3

The Network
Operating System

As important as hardware is to a LAN, it is not usually the most important factor in choosing a LAN. Instead, LANs are usually chosen for the depth and richness of features and services they bring to their users. These features and services are affected by physical constraints, but defined by software: the sets of coded instructions that make your hardware "go" and make LANs (not to mention everything else for which you use your PC) possible. In PCs and LANs, the most important software is that which comprises the operating system.

*W*hat an Operating System Is and Does

Every body has many unique features, but your body doesn't really become you until your mind and personality make their contributions. You might say that your mind and emotions are the operating system that turn your physical components into a complete person.

In the same way, a computer's operating system software tells the various pieces of hardware in that computer that all the other components are present and working, so they can function in concert as a computer. Without an operating system, your desktop computer wouldn't "know enough" to run your favorite application. However, as anyone with IBM-compatible and Macintosh computers in the same workplace knows, one computer's operating system can't always read software or files designed for another.

In the IBM-compatible PC world, the operating system of choice is usually called *DOS*, for *disk operating system*. True IBM PCs usually run PC-DOS, whereas compatibles usually run MS-DOS. The same company, Microsoft, developed both versions of DOS, and the differences between the two are more related to copyright laws than important functions.

Macintosh computers use the Macintosh operating system (usually just called "the system" by Macintosh enthusiasts) and a companion program called the Finder. Some desktop computing systems use an operating system called UNIX, which was designed for large systems and has been adapted for today's desktop systems as well. UNIX is discussed in more detail in Chapters 6 and 9. Other operating systems also are used today, but DOS and the Macintosh system are the most common operating systems found running the hardware on computer users' desks.

Operating systems differ in how they work and present information to you, but they all perform the same types of functions. Operating systems provide a range of services, most of which concern access to your favorite applications, files, printers, and other resources. They also provide a number of tools, or *utilities*, designed to perform tasks that help you make better use of your computer. These tasks range from listing, copying, moving, and deleting files to formatting disks for information storage to clearing your display screen.

However, you can probably imagine at least a few functions and services necessary in LANs that are not necessary for single-computer computing. For example, independent PCs don't have to communicate constantly with other similar systems, but those on a LAN do. A PC's basic operating system is not up to the challenge of managing several PCs connected into a LAN—thus, the *network operating system.*

The Network Operating System: Your LAN's Heart and Soul

In its simplest form, a network operating system works with the operating system of each PC on a LAN to add the missing abilities a network needs. For example, when you use a word processing program on a LAN, your PC's operating system behaves as it did before the LAN. However, it is the LAN operating system software that manages your access to the word processing program itself, a single copy of which is usually kept on the file server and shared by everyone on the LAN. Most basic network operating systems support only one type of PC, because they are so closely linked to a specific PC operating system.

More sophisticated network operating systems use more elaborate techniques to add network functions to PCs without inflicting great changes upon how PC users operate their systems. These more complex software offerings sometimes actually replace the operating system of each server with software that provides both a wide variety of network services and connections to a wide variety of desktop systems.

Advanced network operating systems may also run on or support connections to mainframes, minicomputers, or so-called supercomputers.

Both standard and advanced LAN operating systems usually offer the same basic network-related features. For example, the network operating system typically provides some method of file locking to prevent access to files by more than one person at a time. Without such a safeguard, you and a colleague might try to edit a contract with a prospective client at the same time. This could result in only one person's changes being saved in the final version of the file, or in failure of the entire LAN. The file-locking software feature keeps track of each file in use and makes sure that no file is edited by more than one person at a time. Files can sometimes be locked by personal passwords as well, thus keeping private files private, even when they're stored on a shared storage device. (More about password protection methods appears in Chapter 4.)

Network operating system software also manages connections between LAN users and LAN printers. The LAN operating system keeps track of every available printer and every user's print requests. The print server software in the network operating system then manages fulfillment of those requests, making it appear to each PC's operating system that the desired printer were connected directly to that PC.

The network operating system also manages communications between each network device and its adapter, and among all the network adapters themselves. Priority of access to a shared communications cable or other medium is also governed via *access methods* implemented in network operating system software.

Through various security features, a network operating system also manages each user's rights and privileges on that network and access to other networks as well. (Network security issues are discussed in depth in Chapter 4.)

So a network operating system is basically a manager of connections and resources and a director of traffic among the components of a PC or among the various PCs and other devices on a LAN. To perform these tasks well, today's network operating systems often come equipped with broad lists of features focused on two areas: extensive support of a wide range of connections, and comprehensive network management. Each of these is worth a closer look.

LAN Access: Protocols and Standards

LAN operating systems can be categorized in various ways. For example, some LAN system software is written for specific applications, such as control of various processes in a laboratory or manufacturing facility. In comparison, most LAN operating systems are general purpose, written to support a variety of applications.

Another useful distinction is between LAN operating systems that are *closed* and those that are *open*. Closed LANs are typically restricted to equipment and software from one or a few vendors. These LANs are usually based on proprietary data communications methods as well. The applications and features these LANs can support, and managers' ability to expand them, may be limited by the whims of a particular LAN operating system vendor. Fortunately, closed LANs are now used largely for specific applications. Every major general-purpose LAN operating system now supports some level of openness.

A superior network operating system provides its services and performs its tasks so that you need make only minimal changes in the ways you worked before being connected to a LAN. To do this, a network operating system must support a wide variety of desktop PCs, terminals, workstations, and operating systems. Otherwise, everyone would have to switch to the same type of desktop computer before a network could be built.

In "the old days" of LANs, for example, an Apple Macintosh user working among a majority of IBM PC users had to choose either to surrender the Macintosh computer's ease of use for the uncommunicative A> or C> prompt of DOS or be shut out of the IBM-compatible LAN.

To avoid such conflicts, developers of advanced network operating system are constantly improving their offerings to allow easy connections among a wide variety of user workstations. That's why Novell's NetWare, originally written for IBM PCs and compatibles, was enhanced to include Macintosh support in 1988. It's also why TOPS, originally a network almost exclusively for Macintosh LANs, now supports IBM-compatible PCs as well.

Different types of computers often use different types of network adapters for their physical connections, as discussed in Chapter 2. On the software side, for a network operating system to support a variety of computers, it must learn to "speak" a variety of computing languages, just as a United Nations ambassador or translator must be facile with several human tongues. In computer communications, these languages are called *protocols*.

A protocol, like a language, is not so much a set of words as it is a set of rules for sharing information. Sometimes a manufacturer of computing systems or LANs chooses to design a brand-new proprietary communications protocol. If that manufacturer is very influential, like IBM or Apple Computer, other manufacturers may choose to support that manufacturer's protocols in their own products. With sufficient support from other vendors and users, a proprietary protocol can become a de facto *standard* for the entire industry.

Sometimes communications protocols are suggested by groups of representatives from many industries for adoption as "true" or "open" standards. Such groups are called *standards bodies*, and among them are organizations that may be familiar to you, such as the ISO (the International Standards Organization) or the NIST (the National Institute for Standards and Technology, formerly the National Bureau of Standards, or NBS). Standards endorsed by such groups are often perceived as "more standard" than vendor-developed de facto standards, as they are not dominated by any particular company's priorities.

The computing industry changes rapidly, but the development of communications protocols and their promotion and acceptance as standards takes a long time. Therefore, at the same time that some protocols, from both vendors and standards bodies, are already well-established, industry-wide, open standards, new protocols are emerging and jockeying for acceptance in the LAN industry (and in many other segments of the computing marketplace).

*P*rotocols and Standards in Real Life

Here's a real-life example of the differences nonproprietary, standard protocols can make. Two colleagues in an office use identical PCs for word processing. However, one uses the WordPerfect word processing program, and the other uses the WordStar word processing program. When the WordPerfect user wants to edit a file created by the WordStar user, both users discover that to the WordStar software, a file edited with the WordPerfect program is full of strange characters and format errors.

This is because the two programs use different, proprietary, incompatible file formats. Each program uses different codes to indicate special features, such as bold type or special margins. To share a file, the user of each word processing program must employ file-conversion software, which translates various file formats while retaining most or all of a file's special features. Without file-conversion software, the file to be shared must be saved and edited in *text-only*, *DOS*, or *ASCII* (pronounced *ask-key*) format. All three terms mean the same thing.

ASCII (American Standard Code for Information Exchange) format is an industry standard. When a document is saved as an ASCII file, almost all special formatting is lost, because no recognized, common standards for such features exist. However, all text is preserved, which considerably eases file sharing among users' different programs.

In this example, each proprietary format is standard for its respective program. Although each is popular enough that many other word processing programs support easy conversion to and from its file format, neither program is anything like a universal standard in the word processing market.

ASCII, by comparison, is a better example of a true industry-wide standard. In fact, in 1969 the American National Standards Institute (or ANSI), the NIST (when it was the NBS), and related bodies adopted ASCII as the United States' official standard format for information manipulated by computers. The ASCII file format is therefore supported directly or as an option by every major word processing program for desktop PCs, including the WordPerfect and WordStar programs.

A word processing program's file format defines the codes that indicate a file's beginning, end, size, and other characteristics, as well as information about the format of the text itself. Similarly, a communications protocol defines rules for setting up and terminating a communications connection, beginning and ending a transaction, formatting the communicated information, controlling access to communications facilities, and so on.

As you may already know, dozens of protocols are in use on computing and communications networks. Almost all of IBM's larger computer systems depend on what could be considered a coordinated set (or suite) of protocols, known as Systems Network Architecture, or SNA. IBM has also begun implementing Systems Applications Architecture (SAA), with which IBM intends to link applications that run on all of its computers, from PCs and LANs to its largest mainframes.

For wide-area and international networks, you'll often hear about a protocol known as X.25, which defines the rules for a mode of transmission known as packet switching. Protocols, standards, and quasi-standards attempt to govern every aspect of computing and communications, especially in LANs. (Some of those most important to your LAN's future are discussed in Chapter 9.)

Odd as it may seem, the two leaders of the network operating system marketplace, 3Com and Novell, both purvey proprietary operating systems. However, neither firm's offerings can be viewed as closed, and both support broad ranges of PCs, applications, media, and connections to other computing resources. By supporting combinations of proprietary and industry-standard protocols, network operating system vendors are able to support sufficiently diverse connections to ensure the interest of a wide variety of potential buyers.

Media Access Methods: Essential Protocols for LANs

Chapter 2 discussed various topologies for network cabling. However, LANs require some method for controlling access to the media shared by all the connected devices. Otherwise, a LAN would be like a telephone system in which everyone just picked up a phone, shouted messages into a common line, and hoped the desired listeners heard them.

In fact, a worldwide system of assigned telephone numbers and area codes governs our access to shared communications facilities. Similarly, LAN operating systems manage access to network media. Many LAN operating systems support several different access methods to ease operation on a variety of media, regardless of the topology of those media.

Some network access methods are *random*, allowing any connected device to request access to the shared medium at any time. In comparison, some access methods are *deterministic*, using sets of predefined rules and conditions to assign access priority to the various devices on a network. Some applications, such as process control, and some types of networks, such as IBM's SNA, require deterministic access. Most office LANs depend on various forms of random access, although some do allow network managers to assign priorities to certain classes of users.

Several different random and deterministic access methods are available. The two used in LANs most frequently are the *CMSA/CD* (or *carrier-sense, multiple-access/collision-detection*) and *token-ring* access methods.

CSMA/CD: The Polite Protocol

The Ethernet protocol CSMA/CD is perhaps the best-known access method for LANs. It is an implementation of the carrier-sense, multiple-access/collision-detection access protocol. The Institute of Electrical and Electronic Engineers, or IEEE, a professional association and developer of industry standards, designates this protocol as 802.3.

As its name attempts to imply, with CMSA/CD each connected device "listens" to the network before transmitting information, to make sure a clear channel is available. Only when the network is quiet does the listening device begin transmitting information, divided into regularly formatted segments called *packets*. Each packet is like a letter in an envelope in that transmitted information is accompanied by information about its origin, destination, and location in a particular message.

Although each connected device is instructed to listen before transmitting, the size of a LAN can mean that a just-transmitted packet is too far away for a listening device to hear. If that device then begins transmitting, collisions between packets could occur, resulting in lost or scrambled information and network delays as the errors are corrected.

With CMSA/CD, when a collision is detected, each device that was attempting to transmit is instructed to wait a unique and random length of time and then to retransmit its information. This wait period usually is sufficient to eliminate problems of contention for access, even on heavily used LANs. CMSA/CD also makes very efficient use of available transmission *bandwidth*, or capacity. These features all contribute to relatively low per-connection costs for LANs that use the CMSA/CD access protocol.

Access via Tokens

Another type of access method uses software to create a *token*, or a type of flag, that can be passed along a LAN from device to device. With token passing, only the device with the token can transmit at any one time. A connected device receives a token, sends its transmission, and then passes the token to the next connected device.

Whereas CMSA/CD provides random access, token passing guarantees that every connected device has access to the shared transmission medium within a certain amount of time. Network operating system software can be written to allow manipulation of the rules that govern token passing in a network. For example, different access priorities can be assigned to different network users, based on any number of criteria.

Token passing is used in networks that use bus or ring topologies. In bus networks, all connected stations listen to all messages, and each station responds only to messages sent to its address. Tokens are similarly broadcast, but devices receive and pass them in a logical order, based on those devices' network addresses. In effect, whether the network is a bus or a ring, the token always acts as if it is being passed around a ring.

The token-bus and token-ring access methods have both been designated as standards (802.4 and 802.5, respectively) by the IEEE. Currently, IBM is the leading purveyor of LANs using the token-ring access method. Chapters 6 and 7 contain more information about specific LAN offerings, the access methods they use, and the advantages and disadvantages of each in particular network environments. For now, all you need to know is that CMSA/CD is probably the most widely used access method, though the popularity of the token-ring access method is growing rapidly.

Network Management Tools: Your Network's Best Friends

Another important component of a network operating system is a set of powerful network management tools beyond the file and print service management already discussed and beyond the management of access rights and privileges. Backup, power, and resource management tools are among the most common.

Not every network needs sophisticated backup or power management. However, almost every network does need an operating system that provides and keeps track of basic network information, such as records of who used what program or file and when, and chronological logs of problems and their locations. LANs are growing in number and size faster than the number of people experienced in managing them. Network operating systems with features that help managers manage better are therefore becoming more popular.

*B*ackup Management

For example, some network operating systems can work directly with storage systems designed for making backup copies of network files and other information. The most sophisticated of these systems, which record network archives on everything from disks to video tape to digital audio tape (or DAT), can automatically create and update backup copies of programs, user files, and even the network's image: information such as which users have which rights and privileges, and which servers are serving which groups.

With such extensive backup storage, if a network fails, it can be restored to an almost exact duplicate of its status at the time of the failure. This facility minimizes the amount of work that must be redone and the effects of a network failure. (Procedures for making backup copies efficiently and regularly are discussed in Chapter 5.)

*P*ower Management

LANs also may use backup power systems, just as they may use backup storage systems. Sophisticated network operating systems can also communicate directly with these systems, sometimes called uninterruptible power supplies, or UPSs. These systems combine batteries with circuits that activate the batteries when regular power fades or disappears.

Whether or not a UPS can keep a network operating throughout a power failure depends on the capacity of the batteries, the size of the network, and the duration of the failure.

When a sophisticated UPS detects a condition that makes normal power unreliable, it not only activates its batteries, but it sends a message to the LAN's operating system, warning of an imminent loss of power. The network operating system then begins getting users off the network and updating all backup copies of network information before the UPS itself runs out of power.

Resource Management

In addition to backup and power management, network operating systems can sometimes offer assistance with more traditional management functions as well. Such functions range from keeping track of the number of times users access specific files or programs to helping network managers keep track of users who join, leave, or move around within a LAN.

Perhaps most useful are features that track the rise and fall of network traffic levels and the performance of the network itself. Such information can help managers establish procedures for printing long reports when traffic is light or recommend to users the best times to use large, resource-consuming applications.

Some network operating systems include or support as options software that allows managers to predict the effects on network performance of events such as network growth or the sudden failure of a server. Features like these allow managers to make and keep their LANs reliable and available under almost all conditions. (More network management issues, including ways users can contribute to their networks' reliability, are discussed in Chapter 5.)

What's Most Important?

Network operating systems, like the PCs they connect, vary considerably in price, power, and complexity. Many of the features noted in our whirlwind tour are included in most leading network operating systems today.

Decision makers usually base their LAN purchases on available features, compatibility with systems already in place, overall costs, and similar factors. Because all these elements depend heavily on the strength and depth of an offering's operating system, the importance of this LAN component can't be overstated.

Even though a LAN can be made up of all the elements discussed in this section, when most decision makers talk about buying a LAN, they usually spend the bulk of their time discussing differences among products such as Banyan's VINES, IBM's PC Network or Token-Ring LAN, Novell's NetWare, or 3Com's 3+Open—network operating systems all. Although the operating system alone does not define a LAN, it is the operating system's features and performance that most affect the parts of the LAN that you see and use.

The careful choice of the right LAN operating system is therefore critical to the satisfaction of LAN users, managers, and owners. In addition to the general features discussed in this chapter, your LAN's operating system should support the specific applications and desktop systems users use in your environment now. The less alteration in procedures necessary, the better for users and managers alike.

For most environments, another LAN operating system requirement is support of sufficient varieties of hardware, software, and standards to make the LAN unlikely to be rendered incompatible or obsolete by a sudden shift in user preferences or market forces. Most important, however, is that your LAN operating system, like all the other parts of your LAN, meet your, your colleagues', and your organization's needs. (Needs assessment is discussed in detail in Chapter 7.)

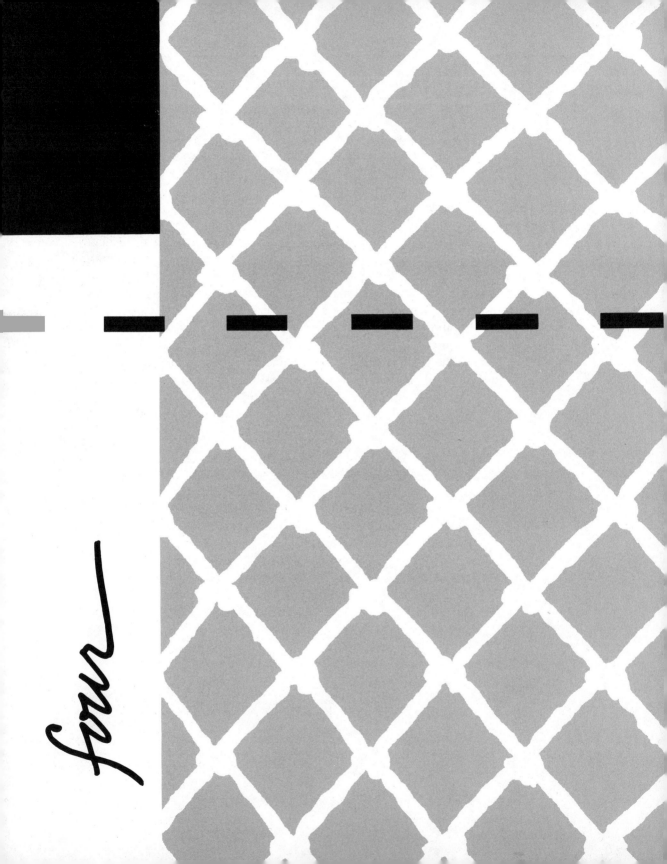

four

4

Network Security

A computing network, like any other valuable, shared resource, is subject to breaches of security. Such breaches can be accidental or intentional, and their effects on network operations can range from harmless to irritating to devastating.

Security is a critical issue to those planning, managing, or using a LAN. It is also a very complex issue. Security is a component of overall network reliability, which is discussed at length in Chapter 5. However, reliability depends largely upon the dependability of network hardware, software, and technology. In contrast, the security of a network depends almost exclusively upon the behavior of that network's authorized users and managers and their guests.

Security, like reliability, is best addressed as part of an overall network strategy. Security concerns must be balanced by other factors that affect the network and its users. Users and managers must therefore discover and implement methods that improve network security without infringing upon users' work patterns or implying that all users are suspected violators of security.

Users have other concerns that network security methods must address as well. Users must be reassured that they can collaborate on projects and share information without being spied upon by managers or other users. Well-implemented password protection schemes can provide much of this reassurance. Managers must also demonstrate to users that procedures for tracking user work patterns on the network are used to improve security and reliability, and not merely to keep a closer eye on users or their activities.

Security methods must be selected with care and implemented with the full cooperation and knowledge of authorized users if security is to be assured. A first step toward these goals is a definition of network security.

What Secure Means

In general, a secure network is one that is resistant to disruptions caused by unauthorized network use. Such a network is designed and operated to minimize unauthorized use and can recover from disruptions easily and completely should unauthorized users evade safeguards.

This general definition of a secure network is a foundation upon which you must build a definition that fits your work group's specific requirements and constraints. An effective definition requires careful needs assessment by you, your colleagues, and your managers. (Needs assessment is discussed in detail in Chapter 7.)

Determining What Secure Means to You and Your LAN

To arrive at a specific definition of security for your LAN, you and your colleagues must first examine your current network or network plans to identify points of vulnerability. Where points of vulnerability occur depends greatly on the work and network use patterns of every member of your work group. An initial challenge thus is to determine these patterns accurately without interfering with them.

If you already have a network, your group will have to decide whether written surveys, personal interviews, software that tracks network access by user, or some other method is best for gathering this information. If you're still in the planning stages, you and your group will have to gather the same information about each independent PC user and use the data to hypothesize points of network vulnerability. A consultant may be helpful with this step.

Every network environment is different, with a different list of specific points of vulnerability. However, most environments have certain vulnerable points. Be sure not to overlook these areas in determining your own environment's particular potential weaknesses.

Securing Workstations and Servers

Like LANs themselves, strategies that address security begin on users' desktops, with their workstations. To protect against both accidental and intentional breaches of network security, users must develop good workstation-protection habits.

One simple habit is turning off workstations when leaving for the evening or weekend, so the screens do not attract wandering eyes and hands. Keeping boot (startup) disks in a nonobvious drawer instead of on a desk or in the workstation's floppy drive also reduces the likelihood of unauthorized access via an authorized user's workstation.

Physical locks are also available for disk drive doors, keyboards, and workstations or PC system units. Some of these locks impede both access and theft. LAN users in large or open-office environments should be encouraged to use these additional security measures and not to defeat them by keeping the keys in their unlocked desks.

It's important to note that in many organizations, the most serious threat to workstation security is not unauthorized users with malicious intent. A larger problem is unauthorized access to user workstations by guests or children of authorized users. These legitimate users often sit their charges in front of an absent user's workstation, to play or explore while the worker works.

This problem is most acute during off hours, when network supervision is minimal or absent. Some companies report a similar problem with after-hours office cleaning staff bringing in and playing unauthorized games on PCs connected to a network. Practices like these must be detected and discouraged to prevent serious network problems caused by well-intended but untrained people.

Servers represent another point of potential vulnerability, especially if they are nondedicated and also used as workstations. As mentioned in Chapter 2, a single-user problem on a combined workstation-server can become a network-wide problem. In addition, even a dedicated server can be mistaken for a workstation if it has a keyboard, floppy disk drive, and a screen attached.

The more critical your network is to your business, the more seriously you and your colleagues must work to secure your servers. Removal of the keyboard from each PC-based server is a good first step. You may also want to put warning signs on servers or to secure them behind locked doors, depending upon their configuration and susceptibility to unauthorized access.

Securing Network Passwords

Another point of vulnerability under direct user supervision is the passwords that allow access to the network itself, as well as to specific resources, such as particular servers, programs, or files. Users remember their passwords better when they choose their own, so assignment of random passwords is to be avoided in most situations. However, users must be encouraged to use a bit of creativity when selecting their passwords to make them difficult for unauthorized users to guess or discover accidentally.

You and your colleagues should choose as passwords random numbers or word combinations that are not obvious, but have enough personal significance to be remembered easily. Such a password is less likely to be guessed or discovered and is a more effective security measure than a password based on your telephone number, your birthday, or a loved one's name.

You and your colleagues must also implement routines for changing your passwords regularly. Some network managers automatically invalidate any passwords more than 30 days old, forcing users to select new ones at least once a month. Your network's security and reliability could be enhanced simultaneously if you and your colleagues changed your personal passwords each time you made complete backup copies of your network files. (Chapter 5 discusses strategies for making and maintaining backup network files.)

Needless to say, some users write down their passwords or store them in some electronic note file. If these users leave these notes where others can find them, all the security you and your colleagues are trying to implement can be rendered useless. Encourage your co-workers to treat their network passwords like credit card numbers or access codes for automated teller machines and to protect them with at least as much vigilance.

Securing Files and Programs

Users can also help protect against unauthorized access to network files and programs. Keep master and boot copies of programs on write-protected disks and, if possible, use passwords to protect your work group's network or application software. When copies of important files are stored on easily removable media such as floppy disks or tape cartridges, restrict access to these media by using locks and keys, sign-in and sign-out lists, supervisor monitoring, or other measures. These practices reduce the possibility of accidental or malicious erasure or modification of important files.

Files must also be protected while they are in use on a network. Users must strive always to open and close files according to the procedures required by their network and application software. Otherwise, network file directories can become incorrect or corrupted, and larger problems can result. Most network software offers some protection against these problems, but good user habits are the best safeguards.

Some network programs require the insertion of key disks into workstation floppy drives to qualify legitimate users for access to programs and files. Where these disks are in use, they must be protected and not widely distributed or duplicated. The use of third-party programs that eliminate the need for key disks must also be weighed against the increased security risk that these disks can represent.

Networks must also be protected from unauthorized programs, such as game programs or other personal software. Unauthorized programs can contaminate your network with annoying or highly destructive software viruses, as discussed in Chapter 5.

You and your colleagues should avoid bringing unauthorized software into contact with your network. Whether a harmless game or your own copy of a program your work group uses, any software not supplied through your network's usual channels should be viewed as a potential source of harm to your network.

*M*anagement-Level Concerns

Managers have a sensitive role in network security. They must help users implement and execute measures like those discussed here and integrate these into network-wide policies that are followed rigorously. These policies also must go beyond the measures that users can implement, but without interfering with users' work.

Managers of sensitive LANs need to address the possibility of their LANs being tapped like telephone lines. With relatively simple electrical devices and a little time, an interloper can tap a LAN cable with little or no immediate evidence. Some LANs can even be tapped from a distance, with devices that monitor the radio-frequency emissions that almost all LANs produce. LANs that permit dial-up connections are particularly susceptible to such taps. LANs based on fiber-optic cable are the most tap resistant.

Call-back modems are security measure used by many managers of dial-up LAN connections. These modems and their software accept user's calls and then instruct users to enter identifying information and to hang up. The modem then checks the user's access information and calls the user back only after the information is verified. Users who enter information that the system cannot verify are refused network access.

Managers must also monitor connections between their LANs and other networks and computers. Managers must periodically audit access to and from network bridges, routers, and other links, and they must regularly update the passwords and other security measures associated with these links. Managers may also have to help users implement more complex personal security measures as their LANs gain access to other networks and systems, and security risks increase.

Managers must also implement measures that provide as much information as possible about network security and about attempted and successful breaches. Ideally, some combination of hardware, software, and physical procedures should be used to provide a near-constant audit of network access and use. This audit will not only help trace the paths of any breaches, but will aid in recovery from any problems these breaches may cause.

Software and procedures that increase accountability can be of great value to a LAN manager and to that manager's organization. Sufficient information about accountability can limit the liability of an individual, a work group, or an organization should an accidental or malicious breach of network security result in a loss of tangible assets or in a lawsuit for some other reason.

LAN managers are also ultimately responsible for maintaining a constant balance between security measures that are effective, and security measures that interfere with users' work patterns or make users feel that their every move is being monitored. The best way to maintain this balance is to involve users actively and positively in the implementation of any security measures.

Users should also be encouraged to see enhanced security as a way of protecting their own livelihoods and work environments, as well as the assets of their enterprise. The LAN manager has primary responsibility for getting both network users and financial decision makers to see network security as a strategic benefit as well as a basic necessity.

In many cases, the best way to enhance network security is to include security-bolstering procedures and tools alongside aids to other aspects of network operation and management. One of the first software products to enhance security gracefully is Certus LAN, from FoundationWare of Cleveland, Ohio. Certus LAN is designed to be invisible to LAN users and can be used to control access to programs and files, to audit network software for changes, to protect networks against viruses, and to facilitate rapid recovery from disk drive and server failures.

For example, Certus LAN can be configured to prevent the running of any software not stored in its list of approved programs. Certus LAN will prevent the software from running, whether the software is loaded from a server's hard disk drive or from a workstation's floppy drive. If a program has been changed in any way since its installation, Certus LAN also will prohibit users from running the software and will warn advanced users or supervisors before allowing them to run it. If a program causes a disk failure, Certus LAN's activity-tracking software allows recovery to the point just before the failure.

Certus LAN exemplifies many of the criteria for effective network security. It is unobtrusive to users and offers sufficient benefits beyond security to encourage its use by both naive and experienced users. Combinations of features like these will eventually be found in numerous software products and perhaps built into future LAN operating systems themselves.

*C*onclusions

Every expert in home, automobile, or business security is quick to point out that there is no lock that cannot be picked, given sufficient time and inclination. The incentive behind sophisticated locks, and policies that encourage and enforce their use, is therefore to make a given facility as difficult and daunting as possible to a potential thief.

Sound network security schemes must accomplish similar goals: They must deter potentially malicious users. In addition, they must encourage users to "lock" their LANs like they lock their cars and buildings. LAN security strategies must also protect networks from nonmalicious, accidental incursions, especially by those inexperienced with LANs.

Technology alone is inadequate to ensure security. True network security is a human issue, with responsibility divided between users and managers, just as network processing is increasingly divided between clients and servers. If viewed as a type of client-server risk management, security naturally becomes part of a larger network strategy to ensure total network reliability and to encourage users to participate actively in the protection of their vital network assets.

five

5

Using and Maintaining Your Network

Before you and your work group commit yourselves to a LAN, you should understand what such a commitment entails. A LAN is more than just a group of PCs and requires more consideration and effort to use and operate successfully.

The connectivity that defines a LAN also increases the complexity of the work group environment for users and managers alike. Both users and managers must change the ways they perform certain tasks, as well as perform some entirely new tasks, all because what were once separate—their PCs—are now connected.

This chapter focuses on some specific issues related to the sharing of information. It also discusses support, problems, and problem solving in an environment that includes a LAN. By considering these issues before you choose a LAN, you and your colleagues can increase the likelihood of choosing a solution that can be integrated into your organization smoothly and completely.

Your LAN and True Information Sharing

LAN vendors often tout the power of their offerings to link numerous PCs and to support additional links to other LANs, mainframe computers, minicomputers, and the like. However, this is only half of the story of shared computing resources.

After all, the real reason for LANs is not to link lots of computers, but to help users easily share information and collaborate electronically. Because vendors have tended to focus more on links among computers and less on links among users, a growing number of users continue to find their LANs to be partial solutions at best.

For example, because a LAN connects a Macintosh user's PC with a colleague's IBM-compatible system, the Macintosh user can easily send her colleague an electronic file, and vice versa. However, because the two users are likely using completely different word processing programs, the file received will probably need editing and reformatting before it can be used easily. This problem is like the one used to illustrate the rationale for protocols and standards in Chapter 3, but it is magnified when both PCs and software programs are different.

Thus, LAN users discover that easier communication doesn't always guarantee easier information sharing or collaboration. In the preceding example, the two colleagues can either use word processing programs that already read and write the same file formats, or they can translate all their files to ASCII code and then heavily edit the files (because when translated, ASCII files lose almost all their special formatting).

This critical issue of how best to facilitate real information sharing must be addressed before a LAN solution is chosen. Not only must users and managers determine the best methods for linking their computing resources, but they must determine the best methods for actually exchanging information among users of those resources.

Fortunately, purveyors of network operating systems and application programs increasingly are addressing this problem. Numerous separate programs aid in the translation of files from one format to another, as mentioned in Chapter 3. In addition, leading application providers have begun integrating into their offerings features that facilitate information sharing.

In the Macintosh world, Claris Corporation began in late 1989 to ship versions of its popular MacWrite II word processing software enhanced with something Claris calls the XTND architecture. This enhancement allows MacWrite II users to open files originally created in other formats as easily as files created with MacWrite II.

To create a file in a foreign format, users simply pick the usual Save As menu option and then select a file format from a list of more than 30 choices. Formats supported include many popular among users of mainframes, minicomputers, and dedicated word processing systems.

To encourage broad support by multiple vendors, Claris makes XTND development tools available to other software makers at no charge. Claris also works closely with a company called DataViz, that makes similar file translation tools used primarily in the IBM-compatible world. The two companies together are expanding the types of file formats supported by the XTND architecture and facilitating development of DOS-based, XTND-compatible software.

The XTND architecture allows LAN builders to use a Macintosh computer and XTND-compatible software as a file-translation server. Equipped with a 3.5-inch drive that can read and write in DOS and Macintosh formats, the Macintosh server can be used to provide file-translation service, even to PCs not connected to the LAN.

Lotus Development Corporation, purveyors of the 1-2-3 spreadsheet, promotes a conceptually similar architecture called DataLens that allows 1-2-3 users easy access to a variety of database file formats. As versions of 1-2-3 for mainframes and minicomputers become more popular and Lotus expands the number of file formats accessible via DataLens, this architecture could become valuable to LAN builders who need access to a variety of databases and who support users already familiar with the 1-2-3 interface.

XTND and DataLens represent potentially exciting solutions to a problem that LANs begin to correct, but don't correct completely. Getting information to the desktops of the users who want it is what LANs do best, but industry-wide acceptance of tools like XTND and DataLens is needed to make that information instantly usable by all.

As with communications protocols, standards for file formats and information sharing are evolving and will eventually solidify. In the meantime, solutions will have to come from high-visibility vendors such as Lotus and Claris. To be prepared for the future, LAN users and managers should begin watching developments in information sharing now.

Developing Client-Server Computing

LANs and tools for easy information exchange are important steps toward client-server computing. In a client-server environment, every user's desktop system is a client connected via a network to a variety of servers that oversee specific resources, such as databases, communications facilities, and applications.

In a client-server system, every client has equally easy and complete access to all network resources (within the restrictions imposed by network managers), no matter where the server that manages those resources is located or the type of system being used as a client. Each client workstation performs the tasks needed by individual users, and processing related to resource sharing occurs at the servers.

The typical LAN is not yet a perfect example of client-server computing, though such facilities as XTND and DataLens are spurring evolution. A LAN that provides client-server computing brings valuable benefits to its users, not the least of which is easier access to more powerful resources.

You'll be hearing more about client-server computing during the next few years, as well as elsewhere in this book. Meanwhile, you and your colleagues should develop clear ideas about what information needs sharing, and how to share it, before you commit yourselves to any particular LAN. Connections alone don't guarantee easy access for everyone.

Your Role in Your Network's Documentation

Almost every LAN user—like almost every PC user—has a horror story to tell about documentation, the instructions supplied with computer hardware and software. Because LANs are more complex than PCs, documentation for LAN components and applications tends to be more complex than that for independent PCs—though some LAN vendors tout the brevity of their documentation as an advantage over competitors' offerings.

In addition, most documentation for LAN products says little, if anything, about those products' interoperation with other offerings. Because LAN products are meant to be connected with other products, this lack is particularly frustrating to users.

Even documentation that is complete can be a mixed blessing. Too often, manuals describe products feature by feature, instead of describing the steps needed to complete specific tasks. In word processing, for example, more manuals contain sections such as "The LOAD Command and How It Works" than sections such as "What to Do to Create a One-Page Letter."

This situation has created a clear need, and an opportunity. The need is for documentation that is concise, clearly written, and truly useful in the real LAN world. The opportunity is for you and your colleagues to compile documentation that works for you.

Creating Personal Documentation

Your first step in creating appropriate documentation is to identify the tasks that are specific to your personal day-to-day work and to document them, just for you. A single page of text, with paragraphs headed

"Starting My System," "Getting on to the Network," and "Turning Everything Off," could contain all the steps necessary to get you started with your most important LAN-related tasks.

After you've written a first draft, try turning off your system and then starting it following your own instructions. This procedure will help ensure that you've included every step and every necessary instruction within each step.

There are two compelling reasons for creating a simple set of instructions for yourself, even though you already know how to use your system. First, should you ever momentarily forget a particular step, command, or option, you won't have to search through a stack of manuals to find the lost information. Second, should you ever need to grant someone emergency access to your part of the LAN in your absence, these instructions will be invaluable.

(Your personal instructions should *not* include your network passwords. If they do, anyone who finds the instructions can gain access to your LAN. The instructions should be readily accessible to anyone in your group, but your passwords should be available only directly from you or your LAN administrator.)

Of course, as your network changes, so will the steps you follow to do your work. You should therefore keep an electronic copy of your personal documentation on your desktop system, as well as a paper copy in your files or on the wall above your PC. This will let you update your instructions easily and quickly.

You should also date each revised copy. That way, if following your instructions produces unexpected results, you can tell if your instructions have been rendered obsolete by changes made in your LAN by the LAN manager. (If you're following your most recent instructions carefully, the network still misbehaves, and your LAN manager claims no changes have been made, either your instructions are in error or you have uncovered a network problem.)

As you can see, the creation and maintenance of your own personal documentation can be helpful in many ways. In addition, it will help you create and maintain other distillations of documentation in collaboration with your colleagues.

Creating Task-Specific Documentation

After you've created your own personal documentation, your next step is creation of instructions for performing specific tasks. Your focus should be on tasks common to most LAN users within your workgroup, but beyond those discussed in your personal documentation.

The tasks to be documented can range from formatting floppy disks to creating network log-in scripts or frequently used types of documents and files. They can also include appropriate responses to specific error messages or other unexpected network behavior. Procedures for making regular backup copies of network information should also be included (and will be discussed at length later in this chapter).

Task-specific documentation is a collaborative effort that produces rewards for all participants. It can help share the knowledge and experience of each member of your group with the entire group. It will also help you bring new members of your network "up to speed" as quickly as possible with a minimum of disruption.

To start, take a look at those tasks you and your colleagues perform most frequently or deem most important. Pay particular attention to tasks that involve the use of several different programs or network components. Task-specific documentation is most helpful when it eliminates the need to open several different manuals to complete one task.

Next, try to reduce the information needed to perform a task to one or two single pages of text per task. Pretend you're writing for someone who's never seen the original documentation for your LAN's components. Draw on the experience of creating your personal documentation.

Be sure that your group's documentation includes any important tips or shortcuts you or your colleagues have discovered after using your LAN for a while. Also include any noteworthy idiosyncrasies of your LAN or its components. For example, late afternoon may not be a good time to send long reports to the laser printer, because everyone is printing the letters that must go out with the day's last mail pick-up.

Inclusion of this kind of knowledge in your task-specific documentation will help both new and experienced users get more work done better and faster. This is the sort of valuable information you'll never find in your LAN product documentation.

The odds are very good that you and your colleagues did not design or build the LAN products you use. The documentation you produce will therefore emphasize how to do useful work, not product features.

Like your personal documentation, task-specific documentation will reward you and your colleagues for your efforts. It will also help you develop procedures for creating and maintaining the third critical component of custom LAN documentation: site-specific documentation.

Creating Site-Specific Documentation

Site-specific documentation explains considerations and constraints related to the role of your work group's LAN within the entire organization. For example, your group may reside in one of several buildings that comprise your organization's "campus," or your group may be in one of your enterprise's many far-flung locations. Your group may regularly need to interact with other work groups or enterprises, including clients of your firm.

How the computing resources at these other facilities compare to those at your location and whether these resources are available to you and your group are important information specific to those at your site. Thus, you also need site-specific documentation that places your work group's LAN and computing resources within a larger context.

Site-specific documentation can begin as a simple list of all the computing resources at your site and their physical locations (with labeled maps, if appropriate). This documentation will help users find the printer to which they've sent a document, especially if they've had to use an alternative printer because their usual choice is unavailable. It will also help staff locate network components for new users and for service technicians lost in a layrinth of identical-looking offices. Remember that some service calls are charged for by the hour, so every minute of a service technician's time can count to your group's budget.

Along with each component's location, information about its functions, capacities, and limitations may be helpful. For example, if a network gateway to remote services is available to your site only during certain hours (to control long-distance costs perhaps), you should include this information in the documentation that describes access to that gateway.

Similarly, site-specific documentation could include general information about your group's LANs, the other LANs in groups around you, and the types of connections and interactions users in your group can expect.

Site-specific documentation might even contain a telephone directory listing who to contact when LAN problems arise. These people should be listed in the order in which they should be called. For those who are not members of your organization, include the name of the organization for which they work, their hours of availability, the amount of time they typically take to arrive after a call, and their usual cost per service call. If service calls are covered by a service agreement, include the number of that agreement with the contact information.

Site-specific documentation is an important complement to personal and task-specific guidelines. It tells users what they need to know before using the resources available to your group and reduces the frequency of network problems caused or worsened by user errors. It provides easy access to information specific to your site that is valuable during identification and resolution of network problems, a topic discussed further later in this chapter.

In short, your site-specific documentation ought to contain less about how to perform tasks than your personal or task-specific information. Site-specific documentation ought to consolidate information about the computing resources accessible from your work group's site, the constraints on the availability of these resources, and the procedures used from your site for the resolution of network problems. This is information only you and your colleagues can collect and manage effectively.

*H*ow to Do It

Even if you're convinced of the importance of personal, task-specific, and site-specific documentation and are eager to get started, you may wonder how you can create all this documentation while still doing your regular work. There are several simple steps you can take to smooth your path toward better documentation for your LAN.

An important early step is to gain the support of your colleagues and network managers. Aside from touting the benefits that have been explained here, you can also demonstrate some of them, by creating and using your own personal documentation. After you've created documentation that works well for you, show it to your co-workers and try to get them on the bandwagon. Get your LAN manager to help you sell the concept to your colleagues, or vice-versa.

To do all this as painlessly as possible, use the technology at hand to help you. Your task can be eased by capturing relevant items as they occur to you, rather than sitting down cold and trying to write documentation from scratch.

Try creating some note files with your word processing software or using a pop-up (memory-resident) note-taking tool such as like Borland's SideKick Plus or FutureSoft's Right-Hand Man. If you're more comfortable with paper files, use those. If you spot some important detail while reading a manual or performing a task, open the appropriate file and add some notes to it. Take time periodically to edit and expand the file. Before you know it, you'll be well on your way toward good personal documentation.

After a while, you and your colleagues can share your files and comment on one another's findings. With a few meetings (and perhaps the occasional group lunch), your group can begin developing common formats for personal documentation and collecting the knowledge that will become the group's task-specific guidelines.

You and your colleagues may find "groupware," or software (such as ForComment) that allows collaborative work on documents, a useful ally in the creation and maintenance of custom documentation. If your group uses shared databases, Macintosh Hypercard stacks or similar tools on IBM-compatible PCs, electronic mail (or bulletin boards), or shared file space, explore using these to help group members easily create and modify the group's documentation "on the fly."

For the creation and maintenance of task- and site-specific documentation, you will likely need your LAN manager's assistance, in addition to his or her support. However, you and your colleagues will have to make participation by your manager easy. Otherwise, your manager may decide the entire project is too much work.

One way to help your manager is to appoint one member of your group as the documentation team leader. This person can be your manager's principal contact, to streamline communications and minimize the amount of time your manager needs to spend on documentation. Instead of attending documentation development meetings, for example, your manager can receive draft materials from the team leader for comments and suggestions.

The key is to look for and use tools and procedures that make custom documentation as easy to create and maintain as possible. The easier the process, the more likely you and your colleagues will be to make the initial effort and to continue it long enough to begin to reap the benefits of documentation tailored just for you and your work group.

Seeking Outside Help

Although custom documentation can be successfully created and maintained by each work group, help from the outside can sometimes be desirable. That help can come in the form of a freelance writer or editor of user documentation, a business or technology journalist, or someone else with documented experience in translating technology into plain English.

If no one in your group knows any potentially appropriate writers, look for advertisements in computing-related magazines. In fact, some of the writers you like in those magazines may be local and available for such work. Make sure to gather and evaluate samples of candidates' writing before testing them with a project of your own. And don't fail to ask them for ideas on how to improve your documentation so you can benefit from their expertise after they're gone.

Your Role in Your Network's Reliability

From time to time, the general press gets wind of a rumor of an imminent attack by a computer virus on some types of computers and networks. Unfortunately, sometimes you'll hear or read of a virus after its attack, when anywhere from a few to thousands of users are affected in ways that range from annoying to devastating.

A computer virus is software that is designed to attach itself invisibly to other, harmless software and to do something when triggered. The virus can be programmed by its creators to become active after its host file or program has been used a specific number of times. A virus can also be rigged to begin its work at a particular time, on a date years after creation of the virus.

Like an influenza virus, a computer virus has the ability to reproduce. It makes copies of itself that attach themselves to otherwise harmless files. Once activated, a computer virus may merely display an annoying and unexpected message on users' screens—or it may promptly reformat every hard and floppy disk it can reach, erasing all the information these media store.

Computer viruses are serious threats to LAN reliability, and they are a symptom of a larger, much more important condition. To the extent that LANs and other computing networks are vulnerable to viruses, they are not as reliable as they should be to support applications critical to the people and organizations that use them.

On a reliable network, resources are always readily accessible to all authorized users. Reliability requires much more than keeping hardware working and providing network security and system passwords. It also includes taking steps to make sure that software remains reliable and user files are always available and up-to-date.

Efficient problem resolution and disaster recovery are also key reliability issues. After all, network problems can be shared as easily as information, with a failure at one user's workstation affecting an entire work group's LAN—and productivity.

To ensure reliability, you and your colleagues must think about it, at least a little, almost all the time. As with liberty and good health, the price of LAN reliability is eternal vigilance. And like health and liberty, reliability has many facets.

LAN managers must reflect concern for reliability in every major network decision. From analysis, planning, and management of the network to the use of redundant (spare) servers and uninterruptable power supplies (or "UPSs"), managers must focus on keeping their networks healthy and reliable. Network security is also an important management concern, and there are dozens of books, magazines, and products on the market to prove it.

As a user, you can't do very much to ensure that your network's hardware and software keep working (although you can help resolve problems, as discussed later). However, you have a clear role in the protection of equally valuable network resources: the files and programs you use to do your work. You can complement the efforts of your network's managers to make your LAN the powerful, accessible tool you want and need.

Backup Files: Your First, Best Protection of Reliability

Doctors, celebrities, and others seem to come up with hundreds of new weight-loss plans every year. Two plans endure, however: eat less food and get more exercise. Despite constant searches for alternatives that are easier or more fun, sustained weight loss just doesn't happen for those who don't follow those two recommendations.

Similarly, new tools and systems to protect networks from failure appear almost every month. However, no new technologies can replace or surpass certain procedures for protecting a network. In particular, no network is truly protected without backup files—current, accessible copies of user files, databases, application programs, and other important information that can disappear with a sudden power failure, surge, or other disaster.

There are tools aplenty that your network managers can use to make your network more immune to hardware, software, and electrical problems. Some of these tools are being built into network operating systems themselves, as with Novell's SFT (or system fault-tolerant) versions of NetWare, discussed in Chapter 6. However, no protection is perfect, so you must nevertheless take steps to make recovery from disaster as rapid and complete as possible.

Creating Personal Backup Files

Like custom documentation, making backup copies begins with you, the individual user. After all, whether you work on dozens of computer files in a given day or on a few for several hours, you don't want to lose these without having backup copies. On a network, since you and your colleagues share files, backup copies benefit everyone. Fortunately, personal backup files are simple to make and maintain.

Many applications include a feature that allows you to create macros. A macro is a set of instructions that you activate with one or a few keystrokes. Some applications let you create macros by recording the keystrokes you use to perform a task. Activating the macro then plays back your keystrokes as if you were typing all the keystrokes yourself.

Some applications, such as Borland's SuperKey, allow you to create macros that work with almost any other program. If you want to use such an application, make sure it will work well with your programs and not interfere with your colleagues' work. If you're not sure, contact the company that makes the macro program.

If macros are available to you, you can create a macro that will save a backup copy of each important file you use, every time you pause to save that file during your work. For your word processing application, for example, you can create a macro that saves the current document as usual, saves an additional copy onto a floppy disk, and then returns you to where you were in the document.

By using this macro and saving your work frequently, you always have a current backup copy of the document you're editing. Even if your network fails entirely, you can use your floppy disk to continue your work elsewhere. A similar approach will work for spreadsheets and other files as well. (If your LAN uses diskless worksations, you may want to attach floppy disk drives to them just so you can use such a macro.)

In the event of a problem that disables access to your network, you may not be able to obtain a backup copy of all of your applications. For this reason, you may want to include commands in your macros that save backup copies of your files in ASCII, or plain text, format, in addition to, or instead of, their usual format. Then, should worse come to worst, you will have files that are not perfectly formatted, but at least are usable with almost any editing program.

You can format and label a separate floppy disk for each application you use regularly or for each of your projects. By switching floppy disks as you move among your applications and projects, you will maintain a complete and well-organized set of backup copies of your most important current files while doing your regular work.

If you can name your macros, you can give each a name similar to that of the file it's designed to save—perhaps the file name itself, preceded by an "s" (for *save*). Remember to save your macros, which is a task separate from saving your other files, and to delete those you no longer use frequently. Save backup copies of your macros on floppy disks as well, so you don't have to re-create them if the network fails.

Needless to say, you can create the backup files described in the preceding paragraphs without macros if you're sufficiently diligent. With macros, the task becomes more automatic and less distracting, which means you'll likely make backup copies more often. Whether or not you use macros, though, you should develop a personal backup strategy and use it consistently. If you've ever lost a large, carefully revised, important file, you shouldn't need convincing. If you haven't, ask someone who has—then develop and use a procedure that works for you.

If your PC has a hard disk drive of its own, you must also back up everything on that disk from time to time, onto floppy disks or some other storage medium, such as tape cartridges. Most PC operating systems include commands you can use for this. For example, older versions of DOS come with programs called BACKUP and RESTORE, and newer versions include a program called XCOPY.

Each of these options helps you copy your hard disk contents onto multiple floppy disks, tape, or another hard disk drive, a task you should perform regularly to avoid losing valuable information to a hard disk failure. Appendix A of this book contains step-by-step suggestions for using BACKUP and RESTORE. Your DOS documentation (or *The ABCs of MS-DOS* by Alan R. Miller, also published by SYBEX) explains the XCOPY program included with newer versions of DOS for IBM-compatible PCs.

Programs designed specifically for use in making backup copies are also available from various vendors. Some of these, such as Back-It from Gazelle Systems (in Provo, Utah), are much faster than the programs included with DOS and offer other useful features to justify their cost, which is typically between $75 and $100.

For example, Back-It tells you how many floppy disks you'll need to back up your hard disk and formats the floppy disks as you make the backup copy. DOS, especially in its older incarnations, is not nearly so helpful. You can run out of floppy disks before your backup copy is complete and then have to format more floppy disks on someone else's PC.

In choosing a backup program, note that some backup programs store your backup files in formats that cannot be read or manipulated by DOS or any other software except the backup program itself. You may feel safer using DOS or a program like Back-It, both of which store backup files in a standard, DOS-readable format. This format makes your backup files easier to use as active files, should that be necessary. If your backup files become damaged, they will also be easier to examine and reconstruct if they are in a standard format that DOS can read.

Also, look for a tool that allows you to make selective backup copies. This feature lets you back up only specific files, groups of files, or subdirectories, or only the files that have been changed since the last backup operation. Making selective backup copies can take far less time than always backing up everything.

Some users make complete backup copies of their hard disks monthly, selective backup copies weekly, and backup copies of specific files every day. By integrating these steps into your everyday work, you'll have the assurance of knowing your files and programs are always current and available, even when your network is not.

Making a Team Backup Effort

After developing effective personal backup procedures, the next important step is to coordinate your efforts with those of your colleagues. Your LAN is for sharing files and resources, so responsibility for protection of those resource must be shared by all involved.

First, talk with other work group members to make sure that everyone consistently makes personal backup copies. Trade macros with one another and share tips to make backing up files easier. Then look at what projects, tasks, applications, and files are shared most frequently and which files would cause the greatest disruption if lost.

List all files in order of their importance. Then decide how and how often backup copies of the most important of these files should be made. If a file is shared by only two or three people, these people can be responsible for making the backup files. For any files (and PC-based programs) shared by most or all of the group, however, you need a group approach.

If your LAN already includes tools and procedures used by its managers to make regular, network-wide backup copies, your group may need to worry about only a few files and programs. Be careful, though, that your group makes adequate regular backup copies (on floppy disks) to continue to work on critical projects, even if a failure disables your network's central backup resources. Your group's latest backup copy of its assigned file server or hard disks, for example, could be the only copy readily available after such a failure.

You and your group must also determine a regular schedule for making these backup copies and delegate responsibility for enforcing that schedule and guarding the backup disks. The more shared files there are, the longer each full set of backup copies will take to make, so scheduling and sharing the work is very important.

In an ideal situation, your group would make and maintain multiple sets of backup files, to provide the greatest chances of recovery from a severe failure of your server or hard disk drives. These can be updated in a rotating sequence, so that you needn't take the time to make multiple copies of your complete set of backup files each time you update them. Instead, for example, you can make this week's first backup copy on one set of floppy disks, next week's on another set, and the third week's on another set.

Starting with the fourth week's backup operation, you and your group would then reuse each set of floppy disks, in rotation. Thus, the fourth week's backup operation reuses floppy disks from the first week, the fifth week's backup operation reuses floppy disks from the second week, and so on. Each set of backup floppy disks can be stored in a different location for added protection of your group's shared files. (This rotating backup strategy is valuable for personal hard disk and network-wide backup operations as well.)

You and your group members should adapt and use whatever personal backup tools are appropriate for group backup operations. Gazelle Systems, makers of Back-It for individual users, also manufactures a LAN version of its program. Back-It 4 LAN and similar products from other vendors include such features as access to local and network disk drive volumes, or sections, and direct support of tape drives as well as floppy disks for backup storage.

Another useful feature of such a program is the ability to compress backup files as they are created, allowing each storage device to hold more information. File compression means fewer floppy disks or tape cartridges and fewer times you or a colleague have to swap full and empty disks or tapes. Make sure to look for extensive features to protect the critical information in your backup files against errors during storage and retrieval.

Some network backup software supports creation of routines that create backup copies automatically at times users or managers specify. With a little effort, you can set up your LAN so that the biggest backup jobs require little intervention to initiate regularly and a minimum of effort to complete. Expect to see more products with features like these, and don't hesitate to consider them for your own group.

Another backup tool uses tape drives and software specifically designed for network backup operations. Emerald Systems and GigaTrend

Technologies are the best-known vendors of such systems, which are certified compatible with the leading network operating systems. These systems often depend upon 8-millimeter tape cassettes like those used in home video systems or digital audio tape (DAT) decks.

As with custom documentation, the best strategy for network backup operations includes tools and procedures that make backup operations easy so they can be performed regularly without disrupting the flow of work in your group. As an incentive for following regular backup procedures, consider the horror of losing a large amount of work. Then multiply your horror by the number of users on your network and the number of hours of frustration required to restore the lost work. The creation and maintenance of consistent network backup operations is guaranteed to be easier and less expensive than the task of recovering from such a situation.

Virus Prevention and You

A software virus may never even come near your LAN. However, as your LAN becomes more important to you, your work group, and your organization, reducing any possible risk also increases in importance. It would be terrible to see your LAN destroyed by a malevolent virus that could have been detected and stopped with a little effort.

You have likely already seen many products advertised as software virus "vaccines." These products, designed to guard against viruses, are of limited usefulness, primarily because for every new vaccine, there's probably at least one programmer somewhere developing an entirely new type of virus. Buying repeated upgrades of virus software can be very expensive and bring you no guaranteed additional security, because a virus may appear that your product's programmers missed.

If you work on a PC at home and also use software on that PC that you did not acquire through your work, however, you should consider getting virus-checking software to check disks that are used in your home and office PCs before each use. In such cases, virus-prevention software can contribute to improved protection and LAN reliability.

In fact, as with human viruses, the best solution is prevention. Because viruses enter computer systems primarily by attaching themselves to files and programs, how users add those resources to their LANs must be examined and managed carefully.

If you intend to use any software on a PC connected to a LAN and that software was not supplied to you by your LAN manager, you must take several steps to make sure it is virus free. First, get your software only from known sources and in its original packaging, with registration cards intact. Even if you want to use just a game program and you're not going to put it on the network, tell your LAN administrator about it and make sure the date of its first use is noted.

For more important programs, you can prevent viruses from harming your system by first using the software "in quarantine" on a system not connected to any LAN. If a virus is due to activate immediately, or if the software has any other problem, it can be detected before it affects you and your group's work.

If a program passes an initial quarantine, make backup copies immediately and store them elsewhere, along with notes about the size of each program. If a program changes size, it may have a virus attached and should immediately be removed from your LAN and examined for further clues of contamination.

Some users and LAN managers avoid making backup copies of purchased programs to reduce the risk of spreading an undetected virus. With this approach, the master disks of all programs must be kept in a secure but accessible location to ensure rapid recovery from a network failure or virus infection.

A growing trend—the use of so-called freeware, public-domain software, and shareware—increases the risk of viruses on networks. This software is either made available by its developers at no cost or can be acquired in limited form at low cost and upgraded (at some cost) if users find it useful.

Much of this software is published by individual programmers or very small companies with limited marketing and distribution budgets. These developers often sell these programs exclusively via mail order or distribute them via modem-accessible public bulletin board systems. These distribution channels can be less secure and more susceptible to virus contamination than more traditional software outlets, although a few instances of contaminations at commercial software companies has been reported as well.

Take even greater care with software obtained from alternative software sources when screening it for your LAN. Preferably, use only software acquired directly from reputable sources and not from public bulletin boards.

Fortunately, some publishers of public-domain, freeware, and shareware offerings have recognized people's fears of virus contamination (and of inadequate software). An Association of Shareware Publishers puts its ASP seal on programs published by its members, who agree to conform to the association's guidelines on software quality, safety, and support. This seal is no guarantee, but it is at least a recourse if you have questions or problems.

Although the virus problem may be exaggerated in the press now, it could pose a major dilemma with just a few strategically distributed contaminations. Caution is not the same as paranoia, and it is certainly better to be overly safe than overly sorry about the loss of critical or irreplaceable network information.

Other Ways You Can Make Your LAN More Reliable

In addition to the suggestions provided in preceding sections, you and other users can make further contributions to the overall reliability of your LAN.

One area you can help with is problem resolution, or fixing things after they've broken. One of the problems with problem resolution is that, by nature, it is usually a response to a sudden crisis. Thus, problem resolution is often not well planned and is rarely integrated and codified into a strategy. Instead, users and managers typically try any of several responses to network problems, none of which is a true solution.

For example, LAN users may spend more of each work day solving other users' problems than doing their own work. Or one user or manager may develop a "little black book" that is the only known list of every vendor and service provider for the network. Sometimes, network users live with problems rather than taking the time needed to solve them. In other cases, users or managers avoid potentially powerful new technologies for fear of encountering new problems.

The single solution to all these problems is a strategy for problem resolution that includes participation by every network user. Because not every organization can afford a full-time staff devoted exclusively to solving network problems, a strategy that values every user's contribution to problem avoidance and resolution is of critical importance.

As a user, a first step is to establish and use a problem log and keep it near your PC at all times. Whenever you encounter a problem, note the date, time, and circumstances. Then do what you think is appropriate in response to the problem and note your response and its effects. As your log grows, you can edit and rearrange your information by topics or by specific network components.

This log will help make you more self-sufficient, as it will evolve into personal documentation about common problems and their solutions. The problem logs kept by you and your colleagues will help your network manager identify and solve chronic problems before they lead to network failures. (The logs will also be excellent reality tests of the vendors' claims about their products' reliability and performance.)

Like your personal documentation, keep both on-line and paper copies of your problem log. You may want to write notes on a ruled pad near your PC and transcribe your notes into word processing or database files weekly. Once stored electronically, your log file can be combined with those of your colleagues and distilled into trouble reports for your LAN manager.

Another contribution you can make to LAN reliability is simply to keep track of all the network components you use, both hardware and software. Every connected device on your LAN has a unique logical address. Unfortunately, networks often grow and change so quickly that no one person keeps track of every physical address. In some large organizations, managers would need weeks to compile an accurate map of their LANs, though such a tool can drastically reduce the time and effort needed to isolate and solve many network problems.

Thus, as a user, you can make and maintain a list of all the hardware and software you use that's connected to your work group's LAN. Start by finding out whether someone already has responsibility for keeping such a list. If so, get the most recent version of that person's resource inventory for your PC and compare it to your actual system.

When compiling or editing your resource inventory, be as complete as possible. Include the brand name of each piece of hardware and software and the version number. Include the item's logical address as well. For major components such as servers and shared hard disk drives, also include contacts for problem resolution in this inventory. Some devices ought to have this information on tags attached to the devices themselves.

Make sure to update this information whenever change occurs near you, such as after software, system memory, or network interface upgrades are installed. Like your problem log, this list will aid you and your managers in identifying and solving problems more quickly.

In the largest sense, you have two important contributions to make to the reliability of your LAN. The first is to work with your colleagues and managers to implement and support procedures designed to improve your network. This is especially important with procedures related to network access and backup operations.

Your second major contribution is as a source of real, accurate information about how your network is performing. You and your colleagues are on your network's "front lines" and are best situated to identify problems, potential improvements, and trends. Remember that you will be the first to benefit from the results of these efforts at problem avoidance and network improvement. The better your network, the better and more productive your work and that of your colleagues and managers. (Appendix B contains summaries of specific recommendations for virus prevention and improving network reliability.)

six

6

*What's
Out There:
Some Important
Network
Offerings and
Their Vendors*

So far, we've examined the basic building blocks of LANs and some of the critical issues that must be considered by those planning or using a LAN. In the chapters that follow, we explore the steps involved determining the need for a LAN, some alternatives to LANs, and the future directions of information sharing. In this chapter, we focus on some of the leading types of LAN offerings available today and the companies that supply them.

So many LAN offerings are available that it is impossible to catalog them all here. Instead, this chapter describes some of the most popular offerings in today's LAN marketplace, from complete basic LAN packages to advanced network operating systems. Features and trends that are innovative or likely to be important to you and your colleagues are emphasized.

The connection between products and strategies also is highlighted in this chapter. The evolution of products can provide important clues about vendors' strategies and plans and so is of special interest to managers and users attempting to develop future-proof network strategies.

Finally, this chapter concentrates on key features instead of offering comprehensive lists of features or tutorials. Numerous other books and magazines are available to help you become more familiar with specific products. Examples include *The ABC's of Novell NetWare* by Jeff Woodward and *Mastering Novell NetWare* by Cheryl C. Currid and Craig A. Gillett, both published by SYBEX. Other useful sources of product information are listed in the resource list in Appendix D.

How Basic and Advanced LANs—and the Products that Support Them—Differ

Before we consider LAN offerings themselves, let us take a brief look at some of the key features of the two categories of LANs: basic and advanced.

As explained in Chapters 2 and 3, full-fledged LAN solutions include cabling, network software, and network interface adapters for each desktop computer. Most LAN offerings that meet these criteria can be thought of as either *basic* or *advanced*.

Both basic and advanced LANs support the important features and benefits of computing networks, including sharing of printers, files, and programs and communication and security features. Basic and advanced LANs differ primarily in price, maximum communication speed, complexity, and the additional features—such as easy connection to diverse types of computers and other networks—they can support.

*N*etwork Software Differences

An important difference between basic and advanced LANs is in the network operating system software they use. Operating systems of independent PCs need enhancements to perform network-related functions, as discussed in Chapter 3. For IBM PCs and compatibles, the DOS network extension is called NETBIOS, or network basic input/output system. Most basic LANs use NETBIOS-based software.

In comparison, the network software that supports an advanced LAN is usually a non-DOS operating system, designed differently by each vendor. This operating system provides a powerful suite of network-related functions and services and includes *extensions* that work directly and automatically with both the network operating system and the NETBIOS operating system of IBM-compatible PCs.

The hard disk drives of servers on advanced LANs must be formatted with the network operating systems, and not with DOS. Basic LANs, in comparison, can use DOS-formatted hard disk drives. This means basic LANs can be installed more easily and quickly, often by users or managers instead of dealers or consultants.

Some advanced LAN network software offers several types of extensions for simultaneous connection to different types of desktop computers, such as IBM PCs and Macintosh computers. However, even though an advanced LAN may support several types of PC, not all types may be able to access all network features equally, as discussed later. Most basic LANs avoid this problem by supporting connections to only one type of PC operating system.

Many advanced LAN products described in this chapter are based on OS/2, the newest version of DOS created by Microsoft and IBM. The OS/2 operating system includes many network-related functions that DOS does not, and which advanced LAN operating systems supply. Most DOS-based advanced LANs incorporate or are compatible with

PC-network, a set of DOS enhancements for LANs developed by IBM and Microsoft in the early 1980s. Microsoft's LAN Manager combines with OS/2 to provide a complete foundation for advanced OS/2-based LAN offerings, such as 3Com's 3+Open software discussed later in this chapter.

OS/2 takes advantage of the special powers of the Intel 80386 chip. In particular, this chip allows OS/2 to manage large amounts of system memory, support communication among various computing processes, and perform multiple tasks simultaneously. Thus, network operating systems built upon OS/2 can be far more powerful than built upon its older, less powerful predecessor: DOS. You'll read more about OS/2 later in this chapter, and in Chapter 9.

Hardware Differences

The hardware differences between basic and advanced LANs are less pronounced than the software differences. For example, with most basic LANs, any workstation can also be a server: either a file server or a printer server. Servers do not have to be dedicated and can continue to be used as workstations. Purveyors of most advanced LANs discourage the use of nondedicated servers as workstations (as do many LAN experts). However, the option is nonetheless offered with most advanced LANs. (Dedicated and nondedicated servers are discussed further in Chapter 2. The evolution of network servers is discussed in Chapter 9.)

Although most basic LAN hardware can be installed by users or managers, most advanced LANs are better installed by professional installers or experienced resellers.

Also, most basic LANs can use telephone-type unshielded twisted-pair cabling. Most advanced LANs operate most reliably and efficiently with coaxial cable, although many can be adapted to operate equally well with shielded or unshielded twisted-pair cable.

Cost Differences

Aside from specific features, the most obvious difference between basic and advanced LANs is cost. The importance of cost to managers is obvious, but users ought to pay attention to costs as well. High network costs can limit network availability, growth, and enhancement.

The true costs of a LAN can be as slippery to pin down as it is important to know. Advertisers, when they disclose prices at all, tend to quote prices for "total systems" that include hardware and software and are designed for a fixed number of users. LAN managers, however, tend to focus on the "cost per node" of various LAN alternatives.

Cost per node refers to the cost of connecting each user's workstation (or *node*). This amount usually includes the cost of the workstation's network interface adapter and connecting cable and a share of the cost of the required network software. The per-node cost of most basic LANs is under $500. The per-node cost of an advanced LAN can exceed $2,500.

Every LAN installation has some unique requirements—from the applications to be supported to the type of cabling to be used—that directly affect costs. Any cost information presented in this chapter should therefore be taken as a starting point, not as sufficient data for direct cost comparisons.

Both basic and advanced LANs are sometimes sold via direct mail and telephone (or FAX). Most basic LANs sold via these methods are offered by both manufacturers and resellers. Most advanced LANs sold through these channels are offered only by resellers. As with PC hardware and software, the discounts available through these channels may be dissipated by additional support or service costs—costs that may be avoided by dealing with local resellers. *Caveat emptor*, or let the buyer beware.

Examples of Basic LAN Products

Although most basic LANs share the features outlined in the preceding paragraphs, they can differ widely in the way they implement these features. Some basic LANs are best used only for small work groups or businesses. Other basic LANs can be used in conjunction with more advanced LAN products. This section examines two typical basic LAN products in detail: LANtastic and Invisible Network™. It also discusses basic versions of more advanced products.

LANtastic: A Basic Basic LAN

One very popular, typical basic LAN is LANtastic, from Artisoft. LANtastic uses the same network interface cards for all classes of IBM-compatible PCs. These cards fit into the short card slots found in some XT-class PCs. For use in AT-class systems, only one small jumper (a small object that fits over a set of pins on the card) need be moved. The cables, interface card connectors, and terminator plugs all use the same round, nine-pin connectors used to connect monitors to most DOS-based PCs. The cabling is made up of dual-twisted pairs of copper wire.

LANtastic interface cards include on-board memory and processing chips. These allow LANtastic's NETBIOS-compatible operating system to occupy as little as 2 kilobytes of system memory in a user's PC. Depending on the number of users in a LANtastic network, NETBIOS requires 2 to 12 kilobytes of system memory per user and 32 to 40 kilobytes of system memory per server. These minimal memory requirements leave more system memory for large application programs, which are often the ones for which the network was purchased in the first place.

Once your interface cards and cables are installed, LANtastic's network operating system and related software must be loaded. This is a simple, straightforward process that is accomplished by typing a few simple commands from the DOS prompt. A network profile is then created for each connected PC to define the devices connected to the PC that are accessible to other network users. The profile also determines which users are authorized for network access. Network profiles can be changed with a menu-driven program included with each LANtastic package.

PCs are logged in, or actually connected to the LAN, via a menu-driven program called NET. Commands for logging on to the network can also be included in the AUTOEXEC.BAT file that starts automatically whenever a PC is started. (See your system or DOS documentation for more information about AUTOEXEC.BAT files.) Once the network software is launched, electronic mail, print spooling, and other features are immediately accessible, as are all authorized resources.

LANtastic operates at a speed of 2 megabits per second, compared to the 4- to 16-megabit speeds of most advanced LANs. Although LANtastic is not exceedingly fast, its speed is acceptable for most small-network applications. At a typical cost of under $250 per connected PC, including the network operating system, interface cards, cables, and terminators, LANtastic offers a low-cost basic LAN solution.

Artisoft has added many enhancements to LANtastic since it was introduced. For instance, LANtastic now supports diverse storage peripherals, including Bernoulli boxes (from Iomega Corporation) and CD-ROM drives. The firm also offers free telephone support and optional installation support through its dealers. However, Artisoft's long-term focus will likely be on low-cost, basic LAN solutions that encompass older DOS-based PCs, leaving other vendors to wrestle with newer technologies such as 80386- and 80486-based systems.

Invisible Software: Upwardly Mobile Basic LANs

Invisible Software's products represent a similar, but different, approach to basic LAN services. Like LANtastic, the Invisible Network product family includes half-slot network adapter cards for PC-, XT-, and AT-class IBM-compatibles, dual-twisted-pair cabling, and a network operating system that supports print spooling, access to remote resources, and electronic mail. However, Invisible Software has evolved a slightly broader range of options and a more advanced upgrade path.

The firm's Invisible Network products range in price from about $200 to $400 per computer for speeds ranging from 1.8 to 3 megabits per second. An Invisible Network adapter card is also available for PS/2-class IBM-compatibles equipped with the Micro Channel Architecture. Instead of the nine-pin round connectors, Invisible Network products use telephone-like modular plugs and jacks. Instead of attaching terminator plugs to the ends of their LANs, Invisible Network users adjust switches on their network adapter cards to indicate the first and last computer on each LAN.

Also, Invisible Network adapter cards have no on-board RAM. Instead, the LAN software takes advantage of an XT- or AT-class PC's expanded memory or RAM in excess of the 640 kilobytes that conforms to an industry standard known as version 4.0 of the expanded memory specification (EMS 4.0). PCs based on 80386 chips, which can support more than 640 kilobytes of RAM, can be equipped with software that emulates (or mimics) EMS-compatible RAM. Invisible Network software can also use "shadow RAM," a type of system memory found in some 80286-based IBM-compatibles.

For PCs that have one of these memory enhancements, Invisible Software's NET/30 network operating system requires only 3 kilobytes of memory for each user workstation and 13 kilobytes per server. Without some form of extra memory, each user must reserve 60 kilobytes of system memory for the NET/30 operating system, with 80 kilobytes required for each server.

NET-30 requires only three commands to get started. INSTALL copies the software onto a PC's hard disk drive. LOAD30 starts the software and allows definition of servers and guidelines for file and command redirection. MAP defines guidelines for network access to disk drives and printers. The software also supports network diagnosis, testing, and security features in addition to electronic mail, extensive print queue management, and other features.

Invisible Software also offers Invisible Ethernet, a combination of NET/30 software and an interface card compatible with the Ethernet access method and thin Ethernet cabling. This hardware-software combination costs $400 per computer and operates at 10 megabits per second. However, thin Ethernet cables are $20 per 25-foot cable, and cable terminators are required, at $5 each. This option allows construction of higher-speed LANs with little significant increase in cost or complexity.

Invisible Software also offers software drivers for Novell's NetWare across its entire range of hardware. Thus, any LAN based on Invisible Software products can be upgraded to run any version of NetWare through version 2.12, including ELS Level II. (See the discussion of Novell and NetWare later in this chapter.) Theoretically, any NETBIOS-compatible LAN can run NetWare, but someone must write the appropriate drivers before theory becomes practical reality.

Although only the Invisible Ethernet card operates at speeds competitive with typical Ethernet configurations, these drivers allow economical power upgrades, especially for smaller LANs where 2- to 3-megabit speeds are adequate. The drivers are $100 per site to Invisible Network users and free to users of Invisible Ethernet.

Invisible Software also offers unlimited technical support by telephone and electronic mail, a 30-day money-back guarantee, and a one-year warranty on all its products. Through enhanced support of Novell NetWare, Invisible Software also provides the ability to increase network power with existing cards and cabling.

Invisible Software's products are clearly basic LANs. However, the firm offers clear paths toward advancing technologies such as 80386-based PCs and the Micro Channel Architecture. Such features allow basic LANs to approach functionality equivalent to that of full-blown advanced LANs in some cases.

*O*ther Basic LAN Products

For basic LANs that must integrate DOS-based and Macintosh PCs, TOPS is the solution of choice. TOPS's offerings combine basic LAN features with powerful and easy-to-use electronic mail and the ability to link PCs with other types of computers.

Novell also offers basic LAN products, called ELS (for entry level system) I and II. These products, particularly ELS II, are fairly complete subsets of Novell's more advanced offerings (and depend on Novell's unique, non-DOS operating system), but they are limited in the total possible number of users per LAN, in their access to other computing resources, and in other ways. Similarly, 3Com's EtherSeries products also are basic versions of that firm's primary advanced products.

All of the products discussed in the preceding paragraphs are excellent examples of basic LANs. They support the features most users of shared computing need, including access to shared disks, printers, files, and programs. However, they tend to lack truly smooth growth paths to more advanced solutions. Remember: Network planners never overestimate, and almost always underestimate, the growth their networks will require, and a solution without a growth path could be no solution at all. If you anticipate growth in your network needs, you should choose basic LANs carefully or avoid them in favor of more advanced solutions.

*T*he Leading Advanced LAN Products: NetWare, 3+Open, and Vines

The dominant products in the LAN marketplace are the advanced offerings from Novell, 3Com, and Banyan Systems. These offerings are considered dominant at least as much for their relative longevity and influence on the market as for the shares of the market they hold. A brief look at their similarities and differences will underscore the important features of most advanced LANs.

NetWare: A Cornerstone in the LAN Marketplace

Novell's NetWare product line ranges from the entry-level products mentioned earlier in this chapter to Advanced NetWare 286 and SFT (system fault tolerant) NetWare. These implementations differ primarily in the number of users each server can support; the types of PCs that can be used as servers; and the extent of security, administration, and problem-prevention features.

NetWare features are virtually identical across all implementations of the operating system. The key strength of NetWare is Novell's commitment to supporting the widest possible range of server platforms, network interface cards, and topologies and access methods. Novell has all but left the hardware business, preferring to leave the manufacture of NetWare-compatible servers and adapters to other vendors.

The two products that are the most indicative of Novell's long-term strategy are NetWare 386 and Portable NetWare. NetWare 386 is a version of NetWare revamped to take maximum advantage of the power of the 80386 PC chip. NetWare 386 supports hundreds of users per server, as well as extensive connectivity to other networks and computers. NetWare 386 is also designed to support easy addition of other features offered by Novell or other developers.

Portable NetWare is a version of NetWare written entirely in the C programming language, like the UNIX operating system. It was developed in partnership with NCR of Dayton, Ohio, and Prime Computer of Framingham, Massachusetts, long-time makers of larger computer systems. Simply put, Portable NetWare is a core version of NetWare's features that can easily be adapted to run on almost any minicomputer or mainframe.

Novell has licensed Portable NetWare to numerous vendors, from Hewlett-Packard and Sun Microsystems to NeXT, Inc. (discussed in Chapter 9) and Northern Telecom, a vendor best known for voice and integrated voice and data communications systems. Novell markets Portable NetWare to such vendors as a fully-formed solution for building links to LANs. This plan is part of an overall strategy to allow NetWare 286 and NetWare 386 to operate in concert with the widest possible range of minicomputers and mainframes.

The market dominance of NetWare will help spur the acceptance of NetWare 386 and Portable NetWare over the next few years. Novell's offerings are well accepted by corporate users, and NetWare compatibility is viewed as a must by most vendors. Other LAN offerings may offer different feature combinations, but no other offering comes as close to being a de facto industry standard LAN operating system as NetWare.

3+Open: A Software-Hardware Strategy

3Com's 3+Open network operating system is similarly rich in functionality. However, 3Com's approach to LANs differs from Novell's in two key ways.

First, 3+Open is based on Microsoft's LAN Manager operating system, which 3Com helped to develop, which in turn is based on OS/2, the successor to DOS proposed by Microsoft and IBM. 3+Open is therefore built on a foundation not exclusively proprietary to 3Com. Because of their relationship, 3+Open, IBM's LAN Server, and other LAN Manager-based offerings could become de facto industry standards along with NetWare. 3Com, IBM, and other companies that license LAN Manager must find ways to make their offerings different enough to be distinctive, but compatible enough to remain attractive to groups trying to make separate LANs work together.

Second, 3Com sells servers as well as software. (3+Open runs on both 80286- and 80386-based servers.) Although, like NetWare, the software can be run on PCs used as servers, 3Com claims that its servers are faster and more reliable than simple PCs adapted as servers. This claim is an important consideration in environments with an existing investment in other vendors' servers. The use of 3Com servers for 3+Open versus the use of a variety of servers for NetWare is the most important difference between NetWare and 3+Open.

VINES: A UNIX-Based System

Both NetWare and 3+Open are constantly being enhanced to increase their ability to communicate with resources beyond an individual LAN. In contrast, Banyan Systems' VINES (or virtual networking system) was designed from its inception to support both PC-to-PC communications and links with other remote resources. In contrast to NetWare and 3+Open, VINES is based primarily upon the UNIX operating system, which was designed to support multitasking, multiple users, and access to a wide range of resources. Banyan has combined these strengths of UNIX with the ability to support connections to DOS-based, OS/2-based, UNIX-based, and Macintosh workstations.

To many users and network managers, the greatest strength of VINES is its StreetTalk global naming service, which allows assignment of logical, easily remembered or located names to network users and resources, local or remote. This feature is particularly useful in larger networks, where access to remote resources can get complex.

Another strength of VINES is its easy expandability. A VINES LAN can start with a few users and grow smoothly into a very large network without wholesale replacement of the network operating system.

Despite its strengths, VINES has not garnered the widespread support of NetWare, in part because Novell has been better than Banyan at marketing and support and developing strategic alliances. However, features like global naming have been adopted by Novell and other vendors, a testament to the validity of Banyan's development strategies.

Other Factors in Choosing an Advanced LAN

As the preceding examples illustrate, advanced LANs tend to offer sophisticated implementations of basic LAN features, as well as enhancements primarily related to access to other LANs and systems. As these examples also illustrate, LAN features and enhancements can be implemented in different ways.

When you select LAN products, you must always remember that you are not only making purchases, but agreeing in principle with the view of the future held by the vendors you select. Thus, you should consider that view with at least as much care as you give to comparing specific features and costs.

Where costs are concerned, any advanced LAN offering is likely to cost at least $1,000 per connected node, including network interface card, software, and cabling. Depending on the topology and cabling scheme chosen, this figure can rise considerably. The only useful cost comparisons must be performed for your particular situation by an experienced and trustworthy reseller.

What Products Tell You about the LAN Marketplace

The LAN market is sufficiently mature that certain trends and user requirements have become clear, and vendors are focused on finding ways to comply with these developments. Thus, the similarities among various products often are more obvious and noteworthy than their differences.

A key need is for LAN offerings from different vendors to interoperate, or work well together. A reflection of the importance of this need is the constant reduction of differences among various implementations of Microsoft's LAN Manager and IBM's LAN Server. Though LAN Manager and LAN Server were viewed as less than compatible when first introduced, they have become more interoperable with the passage of time.

In early 1990, 3Com announced that it was adapting its servers to run Novell NetWare. Eventually, some resellers might combine NetWare with 3Com servers, and 3Com may offer servers that can run NetWare and 3+Open simultaneously. This is another example of the effects demands for interoperability can have on vendors' products.

All advanced LAN offerings are also constantly increasing their compatibility with OS/2 and newer PCs, with the TCP/IP protocol suite discussed in Chapter 9, and with other widely used methods for interconnection with larger computers and networks, again increasing the interoperability among the advanced LAN offerings themselves.

To learn in detail the similarities and differences among LAN offerings, users and managers must examine LAN products closely and carefully, preferably in something approximating a real-life environment. However, before reaching this step, those responsible for building and implementing your LAN must make some basic decisions about your own needs and about the marketplace factors most important to you and your colleagues. This process is explained in the next chapter.

seven

7

**Do I Need
a Network,
and If I Do,
What Do I Do Now?**

As you examine the array of available LAN alternatives, you could easily become bewildered. When you consider these options along with all the other important, sometimes complex, LAN issues discussed in this book so far, you may—and should—be asking yourself whether the efforts of implementing a LAN are worth the rewards for you and your work group.

The answer to this question requires the asking of many others, by both LAN users and managers. You've already read about the most important basic components of the typical LAN and about the leading types of LAN offerings. The next chapter discusses alternatives to LANs for work group computing and information sharing. Before choosing a LAN or an alternative, however, you and your colleagues need to stop and consider carefully where you are now and the steps you need to take toward choosing and implementing a solution.

Doing the Right Thing: How to Know That What You're Getting Is What You Need

If you roll a ball along a level surface, it will tend to travel in the direction you rolled it until gravity and friction slow it down. The tendency to keep going the same way at the same speed is called inertia. A type of inertia often affects decisions about how LANs are built and used. Once an initial set of conditions is established, organizations tend to resist change and to keep going along in the same way, for good or for ill.

It's comforting to know that your ball will roll in the direction you roll it. In the days before PCs and LANs, when most networks were made up of the same types of products from the same few vendors, inertia was very safe for network managers. However, as this book and your own experiences may have already shown you, things are very different now, especially for users and managers of desktop computers and LANs. A different perspective is needed.

All too many managers are keeping all too many consultants in business by beginning from the basic premise that their basic premise is correct simply because it's there, or theirs. For example, too many managers call in consultants or other advisors simply to ask questions like "Which LAN should I get?" In many cases, a better basic question is "Should I get a LAN or keep adding to the one I have?" Unless the past is known to have been perfect, simply building upon it is now inadequate for most situations that involve business computing, especially those that involve LANs.

Before buying or expanding a LAN, a LAN manager needs two things: a very good reason and a very good plan. Every situation needs two processes to achieve these goals and to ensure that the computing solutions chosen meet the needs of users and their organizations, today and tomorrow. These processes are called *assessment* and *planning*.

Assessment is like consulting a detailed map before a trip. It shows you clearly where you are, your possible destinations, and the routes available to you. Planning is like the assembly of a well-designed travel itinerary. A good plan indicates the destination you've chosen, the route chosen to get there, what you need to take with you, and how and when to use what you've taken.

To ensure that they continue to suit your needs, assessments and plans must be reviewed and updated regularly, specifically before any significant decisions about resources such as LANs are made. Good assessments and plans help guarantee that you, your managers, and your organization are happy with each important decision about the computing resources available.

As a user, your roles in both processes are absolutely crucial. It's your job to tell those who manage your computing resources what really works as it was supposed to, what doesn't work, what problems occur most often, and anything else that makes you and computing work more effective in your organization.

As a manager, your role is to record this information and use it to develop action items for you and those responsible for solving your network problems. You are also responsible for encouraging users to follow established procedures and to document and report any and all unusual network events.

Planning and assessment involves more work for users and managers that just living with things as they are. However, this extra work may be the key difference between finding a new solution and creating a new problem. Companies and organizations are becoming increasingly dependent upon their computing resources. As such dependence grows, so does the value of PCs, LANs, and applications that are really helpful, reliable, and available whenever you need them.

Assessing Your Needs

Just like a high-quality suit or pair of shoes that doesn't quite fit, a "solution" based on inadequate assessment or planning may look good, but it will never quite satisfy. The fruit of such a solution will also end up being used a lot less than expected, given what the solution cost, just like that ill-fitting clothing. No one buys clothes without trying them on, or at least knowing the right sizes to buy. Your best interests require you to help ensure that similar precautions are taken before a new PC or LAN arrives on your desk.

Needs assessment must begin with a careful, rigorous assessment of your network right now, if you have one, or of the PCs and programs in use independently, if your work group has not yet built its first LAN. In divisions that are parts of larger organizations, managers may have difficulty determining the exact number of PCs, versions of software, and peripheral devices in use. Users must help in the process of developing a clear and accurate picture of the current environment before any useful changes can be made.

The first question you should ask is just what information and resources need sharing in your work group? What methods are already used for sharing this information, and in what ways are these methods inadequate? With a little investigation, you may find that a solution already exists, but has been poorly documented or not considered seriously enough.

Let's say you're part of a group of five colleagues, and you all have PCs. Let's say you don't have a receptionist to answer phone calls, so you all take messages for one another, but accurate messages often fail to reach their destinations. Perhaps you need a LAN with software for taking and delivering telephone messages electronically.

Of course, such a solution requires someone to select the right software, authorize payment for it, get it installed and working, make sure everyone is trained to use it, and so on. On closer inspection of your group's needs, you may find that all you need is more pens and "While You Were Out" notepads.

Not every group of PC-using co-workers needs a LAN, and not every LAN in place is the best available solution. You need to evaluate how what you use now works; keep notes on ideas and questions as they occur to you (perhaps on your PC or LAN); and get colleagues, managers, and vendors to respond to the issues that arise.

On a larger scale, to select the right LAN or non-LAN solution, users and managers need to assess accurately the resources that need sharing and the number of people who will benefit from the sharing—today, in six months, and a year from now. To contribute to these assessments, you may have to consider factors you don't ordinarily think about, especially if you're not an experienced manager of LANs.

It's important to remember that the best needs assessments often begin with basic details. Examples include the number of hours a day you and your colleagues use word processing software versus a spreadsheet program, or how many people are involved in each current project.

The single step of counting such things as hours spent on particular tasks can be extremely important in determining the best LAN solution or alternative for you and your colleagues. Such counting also is something that should be done periodically to help evaluate the effects of changes, such as new versions of applications software, on a work group's solution.

You and your colleagues must also make your best guesses about what you'll need to do personally to help make any proposed change a reality. Will you need to make radical changes in how you use your PC? Will you be able to use the new software easily, or will you and your colleagues need time off for training during some critical project? If you need time off, can it or the project be rescheduled? If not, do you need the software badly enough to offset the difficulties time off creates? These and many other questions demonstrate how you should approach the assessment process when using or building LANs.

Development of a complete assessment, and a process for performing future assessments, is the first task many LAN consultants perform for many of their clients. If you are a manager considering soliciting a consultant's advice on your work group's computing solution, you should discuss the consultant's procedures for assessing your needs and auditing your existing situation. Inquire about the consultant's specific methods, especially as they affect your working colleagues. Will they have to keep logs of their computing use? Will they participate in discussions with the consultant? Will these or other requirements disrupt their work excessively?

A consultant's specific experience in assessments and audits can be valuable information as well, so you should query the consultant about his or her background. A consultant's agreement to perform an assessment does not guarantee sufficient experience to make the assessment valuable to you and your colleagues.

You should also insist that you be allowed to end your relationship with the consultant after the assessment of your environment is completed and delivered. Otherwise, a consultant may be overly motivated to recommend changes that continue a relationship with your group but do not necessarily improve your computing solution.

To be complete, a thorough assessment must consider the computing needs being addressed within the context of the needs of the individuals, groups, and organization involved. These needs range from financial to social and are all essential to accurate assessment and appropriate plans.

In many cases, the only accurate source of information about who needs what are the users and managers of what's actually being used. You must therefore pay attention to how well the solution on your desk really meets your needs and communicate that knowledge to those responsible for the inevitable changes in your computing resources.

*P*lanning Strategically for Effective Solutions

Have you ever missed a delivery or appointment because of an unanticipated delay or because a previous engagement ran too long? Then you already know the value of clear planning to the success of almost anything. Planning is especially important with LANs, if for no other reason than the large number of things that can go wrong.

Good planning anticipates things going wrong. That's why countdowns for NASA rocket launches include blocks of time during which nothing happens. If something goes wrong, these blocks of time can be used for making repairs or adjustments without postponing the scheduled launch time.

Once needs assessment has helped you and your managers choose the solutions most likely to succeed, you must make plans for making a final choice. You should make plans to choose a consultant, choose a reseller, choose an installer, choose among various maintenance and service options, and deal with problems large and small. Has your organization included plans to hire and pay for additions to the LAN management staff, if additions are needed? Have plans been made to locate a good consultant or to solicit recommendations? Are all of your colleagues being kept well-informed about the coming changes?

Users have to make plans as well. Will users' PCs or LANs be out of service while the LAN is being installed or enhanced? If so, what files should be copied onto floppy disks so users can work on them elsewhere and to ensure that critical data isn't destroyed by a problem during the installation?

A critical component of any LAN plan is another assessment, this time of what your proposed solution will cost your department and your organization. You must realize that LANs can cost far more than the total cost of their components, just as employees cost a company more than their salaries because of benefits, training, and similar expenditures. Consultants, extra training, cabling installation, and service or support contracts can add up to multiples of a LAN's component costs. (Cabling planning is discussed later in this chapter.)

Once your work group has chosen a LAN and justified its costs, you and your colleagues must plan for the new network. Do you have lists of all the passwords and other information you need to access the network once it's available? Do you know who has these lists, if you don't? Do you already know the new commands necessary to use the applications you use most often? If not, do you know who does? Has someone among your colleagues been designated the expert on the chosen solution? Is that job going to fall to you or to someone else who already has a busy job?

The user's role in LAN planning is at least as important as the manager's role in assessing needs and resources. Users must help managers determine how to make the solution of choice work and whether the solution is worth its cost. If it is, users must participate in determining and executing the steps necessary to turn a chosen solution into a working benefit.

A few years ago, a well-known software company moved into a new complex. Workers left the old complex on Friday and reported to the new complex the next Monday. Each worker arrived to find a new, up-to-date corporate telephone directory on his or her desk and the phones working. This smooth transition required weeks of planning, training, and coordinating with everyone from the local telephone company to the workers who managed the company's loading docks. At every step, users were informed and consulted about what they needed and what was required of them.

Users must make sure they're included when their organization plans to build or enhance a LAN connected to the PCs on their desks. One major contribution users can make is their knowledge and opinions about the solutions being considered for them and their colleagues. Users should not be timid about letting their voices be heard, and managers should listen carefully to what users have to say.

A Final Caution

LANs are much more intricate than independent PCs. They therefore require more intricate, sophisticated management if they are to meet the needs and expectations of their users, managers, and organizations. You and your work group must decide if you are really ready to acquire the knowledge and skills necessary to operate a LAN before you decide which LAN to get. A simpler solution may not offer as many features, but it may be easier and more cost effective for your group to own and operate than a more sophisticated LAN.

In addition, although consultants and vendors can often be good sources of information, they are not at your work site every day. Someone who is present every day must be appointed to head the "bureau of LAN management," and that person must get the training and support necessary to do the job right. Otherwise, your network could impede rather than improve productivity.

Decisions, Decisions, Decisions

Since the advent of PCs, there have been underused PCs on a lot of desks. To ensure that LANs or other work group computing solutions get maximum use, managers must develop coherent, complete plans that integrate these solutions into existing environments and work practices as efficiently and smoothly as possible. Effective plans are based on careful assessment of needs, current practices, resources, organizational strategies, and other relevant factors, as discussed earlier in this chapter.

In building or changing a LAN or effecting some other work group computing solution, almost every LAN builder faces several basic questions in their assessments and plans. Some of these question are discussed in the following sections. Others are discussed in Chapter 9.

IBM versus IBM-Compatible PCs

If your work group already uses PCs extensively, you've already made some choices about what type or types of systems to put on your desks. For most work groups, the first choice is usually between IBM-manufactured PCs or IBM-compatible PCs manufactured by other companies, some new and small and some large and well-established.

Some may think the primary consideration in choosing between IBM PCs and compatibles, or "clones," is price. For every model of IBM PC, there are at least three nationally known, equivalently configured compatible systems that are significantly less expensive than IBM's own offerings. Depending upon the supplier and the sources of their PC components, manufacturers of compatibles can often undercut IBM's retail prices by 50 percent or more.

However, deciding which PC to use requires consideration of more than price alone. If your work group is part of a large organization that has a significant investment in IBM computing systems, this may be a sufficiently compelling reason to choose IBM-manufactured PCs, both for independent computing and as workstations connected via LANs. Your group may be able to take advantage of contracts your organization already has with suppliers of IBM systems to lower the cost of your IBM PCs and LAN.

There may be other compelling reasons for choosing IBM offerings over compatibles. If IBM or a major reseller of IBM systems has strong support and service resources near your work group, reliability and rapid recovery from problems might be worth the additional expense of IBM-labeled products. However, you should confirm with other local users that the quality of the support is worth the additional expense before eliminating alternatives from consideration.

You should also remember that not all compatibles are less expensive than PCs or LAN products from IBM. PCs and servers from Compaq Computer Corporation, for example, are sometimes more expensive than equivalent systems from IBM. In fairness, Compaq's systems also tend to be faster and more powerful than the IBM offerings that inspire them.

If your work group or organization has no existing investment in computing systems from IBM or some other vendor, you may derive real benefits from buying compatibles from manufacturers other than IBM. In addition to price, some compatible makers incorporate features in their systems that IBM supports only as extra-cost options or not at all. In addition, you and your colleagues may find vendors of compatibles more willing to configure systems to meet your specific needs.

Leading vendors of compatible systems have begun to offer service and support options that rival those available from IBM and other major manufacturers. Most compatible vendors offer their users service contracts with third-party companies that often offer service depots in numerous locations as well as service at the user's site.

The lower prices of IBM-compatible systems sometimes include access to service and support. When they do not, you may want to buy a service contract to help ensure reliability, using a portion of the budget you've saved by choosing compatibles over IBM-labeled systems.

If you choose IBM-compatible offerings over IBM-labeled offerings, you may have more freedom in choosing products to meet specific needs. However, you may have to manage relationships with multiple vendors, manufacturers, and service providers, which may reduce the value of any money you save.

Those who choose compatible offerings sometimes do so to avoid dependence upon IBM's strategic decisions. However, if IBM makes new systems less easy for compatible makers to duplicate and sell at lower prices than IBM's, users of compatibles may find themselves blocked from access to technological advances. IBM's PS/2 line of PCs and OS/2 operating system are evidence of precisely such a situation. In fact, systems compatible with these newer IBM offerings are usually not discounted as steeply as those systems compatible with older IBM PCs. (See Chapter 9 for further discussion of OS/2 and PS/2-class PCs.)

In sum, if your work group or organization has some compelling reason for sticking with IBM-labeled products, you should consider this factor before you make any significant PC or LAN decisions. Take maximum advantage of any existing relationships with IBM or its suppliers to get the best deal for your PCs and LAN products. If your work group is in an organization with a commitment to some other computer manufacturer, such as Hewlett-Packard or AT&T, don't neglect the IBM-compatible systems available from that manufacturer.

If your organization has no compelling commitment to IBM or any other computer vendor, compatible PC systems are worthwhile alternatives, if they are carefully selected and well supported. Many LAN managers who support IBM-compatible PCs buy them from a variety of suppliers to get the best combinations of price, features, and value. Some managers choose to give all their business to one vendor, hoping to garner more influence as a larger account. Select carefully, and don't be afraid to change vendors if you're dissatisfied with support or service.

Because the PC is every user's window to your work group's LAN, the PCs selected should be the best values available, not just the least expensive. With adequate support and the right combination of features, compatibles from reputable vendors can meet this criterion. If you cannot or do not want to perform the additional evaluation and selection tasks necessary when buying compatibles, the apparently more expensive offerings from IBM may, for you, represent the best value.

In many cases, an ideal solution is for managers to create a list of approved IBM and compatible systems and then allow LAN users and managers to select their systems from this list. This procedure lets individuals choose their systems from a range of options and guarantees compatibility and easy integration of individual systems into LANs and other solutions. However, this procedure also requires extensive comparison and evaluation of compatible systems by users and managers.

*D*OS-*Based PCs versus Macintosh Computers*

The computers on the desktops of most business users are IBM-labeled, IBM-compatible, or Apple Macintosh systems. LAN operating system vendors frequently tout connectivity to a variety of systems, but not all LANs bridge the differences between IBM-type and Macintosh systems.

An important factor in building a LAN is ascertaining whether IBM-type or Macintosh systems are dominant in a work group. If neither is dominant, you must determine whether users have a clear preference for one type of system or the other. If they don't, the best LAN solution is one that allows connection of both IBM-type and Macintosh computers.

In work groups where a preference is clear, the best LAN solution is the one that brings the most benefits to the most users. If a work group uses few of one type of PC, a LAN solution that excludes the minority may be sufficiently beneficial to the majority to be justified.

However, LANs almost always change, and change is rarely predictable. There are few situations that would not benefit by implementing solutions that support both IBM-type and Macintosh PCs. This approach avoids the need to build and connect a second LAN should the minority

PC grow in popularity. (More discussion of the Macintosh system appears in Chapter 9.)

Twisted-Pair versus Coaxial Cable

Once you have selected your PCs, you need cabling to connect the PCs to each other and to other resources. The two most popular media are twisted-pair and coaxial cables, as discussed in Chapter 2. Twisted-pair cable is less expensive and easier to install, but is not always preferable to coaxial cable.

Twisted-pair cable is best-suited to a LAN that has relatively few users and low traffic. It's also ideal for LANs implemented on a trial or experimental basis. It's easy to work with and widely supported by many LAN manufacturers.

Coaxial cable, on the other hand, can carry more information further with fewer errors than an equivalent length of twisted-pair cable. Also, coaxial cable comes in forms that can be installed in more types of environments than most common varieties of twisted-pair cable. Some types of twisted-pair cable offer greater data protection than others, but these offer less cost advantages over coaxial cable.

Most LAN builders use the cable recommended by their LAN vendors. However, the specifics of each situation must be examined carefully to discover any potential advantages or cost savings possible with alternative cabling methods. An example of alternatives that require such careful consideration is the class of network offerings that support Ethernet LANs over twisted-pair cabling, instead of the more expensive coaxial cabling used in most traditional Ethernet installations.

Coaxial cable is more expensive than twisted-pair cable and should be installed only by reputable, experienced, bonded installers. Twisted-pair cable can sometimes be installed by managers or users, so it might seem to be the obvious choice for simplest LAN configurations. However, all but the smallest and simplest twisted-pair LANs can benefit from the support of a professional installer. An outside installer also gives you someone to call should you experience cable-related problems.

Some vendors promote the use of in-place telephone wiring, usually made up of twisted-pair cable, as a LAN solution. Using telephone wire is a good idea only if the quality and layout of the in-place wiring can be documented by a manager from your organization or by an outside cabling expert. In general, if in-place wiring is more than a few years old, its quality and ability to carry data reliably is subject to question. It is often less expensive to install new twisted-pair cable than to make in-place wiring work reliably for a LAN.

The trend in the LAN industry appears to be toward use of twisted-pair cable for work group solutions and of coaxial cable (or fiber-optic cable, in some cases) as a backbone that links these smaller LANs in to larger networks. (See Appendix C for a more detailed discussion of issues that affect cabling choices.)

Ethernet versus Token Ring

A popular debate among LAN builders is over the strengths and weaknesses of the Ethernet and IBM Token Ring LAN access methods. Data from market research firms such as International Data Corporation indicates that Token Ring products are sellng at rates rising much faster than those for Ethernet products, indicating that Token Ring LANs could become as popular as Ethernet LANs within a few years.

Supporters of both Token Ring and Ethernet LANs often cite the maximum possible transmission speeds of the technologies as competitive advantages, with the lead changing hands with every technological improvement. In addition, Token Ring adherents also laud the technology's deterministic access scheme as being better suited for some applications than is the random scheme of Ethernet access.

Token Ring fans also point out that Token Ring technology is IBM's declared LAN foundation of the future and an integral part of IBM's broader connectivity strategies, especially those for linking PCs and LANs with larger computers and other networks. Apple Computer has made its LocalTalk network environment directly compatible with Token Ring LANs in apparent recognition of the importance of future compatibility with IBM networks. Third-party offerings that support compatibility with Token Ring LANs abound as well.

Ethernet, in comparison, has the advantages of being established, proven, and well understood, at least in the DOS environment. Direct support of Ethernet is limited in Apple Computer's products, although the need has been met more than adequately by a variety of third-party vendors. In fact, Ethernet can support Macintosh computers so well that servers from Ethernet LAN vendor 3Com are used enthusiastically by developers at Acius, a vendor of Macintosh software founded by former Apple Computer personnel.

Ethernet also uses a bus topology, which some find easier to expand or change than the star topology upon which Token Ring LANs depend. Another advantage for some users is Ethernet's longer history of being run successfully on twisted-pair cabling, instead of on the more expensive coaxial cable recommended for most Token Ring installations.

Lucid technological arguments can be made on both sides. However, LAN choices should not be based so heavily on technological factors. Many other factors, some of which have little to do with the relative merits of the two technologies, need to be considered.

For example, IBM Token Ring network adapter cards are hard to get in many areas of the country, because demand exceeds available supply. As IBM develops newer and higher-speed LAN interface cards, demand for those will likely exceed supply as well, at least for a while after the cards are introduced. Ethernet cards, by comparison, are readily available in most areas. Ethernet cards also tend to be less expensive than Token Ring cards.

Thus, unless you have a compelling reason for implementing a Token Ring LAN, an Ethernet LAN may be a more predictable and economical solution. This situation may change during the mid 1990s, as Token Ring LANs become more widely used and better understood.

*M*aking Other Choices

Another choice facing many LAN builders is between a basic LAN that does not require dedicated servers and a complex LAN that requires dedicated servers. If management resources and LAN requirements are limited, a basic offering may be sufficient. However, if growth or interconnection with other LANs is anticipated, or if your LAN may need new features in the future, remember that server-based LANs are easier for most managers to upgrade or change. (For further information about the differences between systems that require dedicated servers and those that do not, see Chapter 2.)

LAN builders face many other choices and decisions. However, the resolution of fundamental issues such as those raised in this chapter ultimately determines the quality of every work group computing solution and the satisfaction of work group members.

eight

Sharing Resources
without
LANs—or You
May Not Need
a Network After All

The main purpose of a LAN is to share resources. In many cases, computing resources can be shared by implementing solutions that may be less expensive, easier to manage or operate, or otherwise more appropriate to a situation than a full-blown LAN.

Although none of these solutions brings as many benefits to users as a LAN, such a solution may be sufficient for a particular environment, and in addition may be a first step toward full LAN-hood. Most groups of PC users consider LANs and their alternatives so they can share files, electronic storage areas, printers, and programs. This chapter presents some ways to share these resources without a LAN.

Sharing Files, Storage Areas, and Programs

The earliest form of file sharing, still in widespread use, is often known as "SneakerNet." With SneakerNet, you save the file to be shared on a floppy disk, take the disk out of your drive, put on your sneakers, and carry the disk down the hall to the person who needs to share it with you. Your colleague inserts the disk into his or her floppy disk drive and continues working.

Several years ago, someone making a presentation at a computer industry trade show said that the people at his company had found Sneaker-Net to be simpler, more economical, and more reliable than any LAN available at the time. The presenter was Phillipe Kahn, founder and president of Borland International. Borland is the California software company that produces SideKick (a program that provides notepad, calculator, and other goodies that users can "pop up" in the middle of any other program), Sprint (a fast, flexible word processor), and numerous tools for programmers. SneakerNet worked at Borland, and it still works in many environments.

More recently, though, Kahn's image graced magazine ads for Sun Microsystems' TOPS LAN products, and SneakerNet has become a less powerful solution than it used to be. Two factors are the successes of the Macintosh and the 3.5-inch disk drive for newer IBM-compatible PCs, which diminish the likelihood that a disk from your PC's floppy disk drive will even fit into a drive on a colleague's system.

In addition, even if both drives are the same size and both systems are IBM PCs or compatibles, your disk may be written in a format incompatible with your colleague's disk drive. This obstacle occurs because the AT class of IBM PCs and compatibles can read disks from older PCs, but they can't always write disks that those older PCs can read.

For SneakerNet to be truly effective today, every desktop system in a group must be equipped with a disk drive that can read and write disks everyone else can share. This strategy can cost several hundred additional dollars per PC, especially if it involves a 3.5-inch and a 5.25-inch drive for each system, or a 3.5-inch drive from Apple Computer or other vendors that can read and write disks in both IBM-compatible and Macintosh disk formats. This strategy also brings more hardware, and more opportunities for hardware problems, to every user's desk.

A remedy for hardware and software incompatibility is extensive use of software products designed to make file transfers easy, even among machines with incompatible disk drives. Perhaps the best known of these are LapLink Plus, DeskLink, and LapLink Mac, from a company called Traveling Software. These and similar products from other vendors include a length of cable that plugs directly into a port on each of two computers and software that lets you easily transfer files individually or in groups. Newer versions of such products use the parallel ports of linked PCs for faster data transfer. These products often include utilities for conversion among file formats of the more popular applications, such as WordPerfect and Lotus 1-2-3.

Such products can be wonderfully direct and simple solutions for occasional file sharing, especially between Macintosh and IBM PCs or between desktop and portable systems. However, some feel these solutions are too slow or inconvenient for heavy-duty file sharing. In addition, if everyone in the group isn't using exactly the same applications, some file conversion may be necessary.

Thus, enhancements can add value to SneakerNet as an information-sharing alternative. However, SneakerNet is most valuable in environments where almost everyone uses the same type of PC disk drive, and ease of file sharing is more important than such applications as electronic mail.

Another resource that can be shared without LANs is electronic storage space for files and programs. Numerous manufacturers offer portable, external hard disk drives that can be used with one computer and then moved to another computer and used with it (assuming that it is a compatible system and has a compatible interface).

Some years ago, a few manufacturers promoted RAM boxes, portable units full of RAM chips, interface circuitry, and batteries. The RAM chips store data while the RAM box is being carried from place to place. Although RAM boxes offer much faster performance than the fastest portable hard-disk drives, their prices and availability vary with changes in the worldwide memory chip market.

Hard disks small enough to fit on IBM PC-compatible expansion cards are also available, complete with the necessary controller circuitry. These can be used for file sharing among computers, although having to open and close computers and insert and remove the drive cards can be a nuisance and can jostle a drive sufficiently to cause the loss of information.

The sharing of programs can be accomplished with most of the file-sharing alternatives already mentioned. However, most commercial programs are sold to be used by one person, on one computer. Although it's all too common to see users sharing a single copy of a commercial program, this is, in fact, an illegal practice, unless the program has been purchased under terms with no single-user restrictions.

For LANs, managers simply purchase LAN-specific versions of their favorite applications. In alternative solutions, managers must either buy a single-user version of each application for each user and computer or negotiate a volume purchase agreement or site license with the relevant software manufacturers and resellers. Such arrangements usually provide sufficient software to support multiple users or sites at prices lower than those of multiple single-user copies of each program. However, not all software is available under such terms, and arrangements like these are not appropriate for every environment, especially in organizations with few users or large amounts of money already invested in single-user software.

S*haring One Printer—or More*

Sadly, few printers designed for the typical work group come from their manufacturers already equipped to support connection to more than one computer simultaneously. Happily, solutions for sharing printers without LANs abound. Such solutions range from the simple to the complex.

For the sharing of one printer by a few users, the most straightforward solution is the use of software with a print queuing feature. Print queuing collects and stacks users' print requests and executes them one at a time without tying up each user's computer for the duration of printing. Print queuing is available as a separate software offering and is sometimes included in other applications, particularly word processing programs.

A variation on print queuing is the use of printers with built-in buffer memory, which is usually in the form of RAM chips inside the printer case or in a buffer box connected to the printer externally. Buffer memory also queues and executes print requests, even from users of applications without print queuing. Such memory adds to the cost of each printer and is an added potential source of problems.

To share access to a few printers among a few users, a common solution is a variation on SneakerNet. Each desired type of printer is connected to a specific workstation. Anyone who wants to use that printer takes a disk with the file to be printed to that workstation and either interrupts the user of that workstation or waits until that user completes his or her work in progress.

This solution's pluses and minuses are similar to those of SneakerNet. It is likely unworkable in most environments where a full-scale LAN is in use or under consideration. However, this approach definitely is worth considering in environments with only a few PCs, only a few printers, and little to no expectation of significant growth in the number of "connected" users.

Another simple solution is to use a switch box that lets two computers share one printer, or one computer choose from two different printers. Cables are run from the computer(s) to the switch box and from the box to the printer(s). A simple two-position switch is flipped to select the appropriate computer and printer pair. Such switches are available for under $100 from retailers such as Tandy Corporation (which owns the thousands of Radio Shack stores across the United States) and from mail-order office and computer supply houses.

Some users connect several of these simple switch boxes together to allow switching among more computers and printers. This procedure can work, but it is cumbersome. All switch boxes, cables, and printers must be labeled clearly and correctly because users must set all the switches between the workstations and printers they want to use for each and every print request. Moreover, the switches have to remain as set by the user until the print request is fulfilled. Thus, only one user can print at a time. This problem is alleviated somewhat if every printer is equipped with its own *buffer memory*, but this method still is inconvenient. (Buffer memory is some amount of RAM installed directly into a printer instead of on a PC or server. The buffer allows a printer to receive an entire file in one short transmission from a user's PC, so the user can continue performing other tasks while the printer finishes printing. Like print servers, buffer memory keeps print requests from tying up users and their PCs.)

A better approach than connecting multiple simple switch boxes is to use one of the more elaborate switch boxes available to support multiple printers and computers. Tandy Corporation, for example, offers a line of printer-sharing systems known as Easy-PRINT systems. These systems range in capacity from two computers and one printer to six computers and two printers, and they range in price from about $100 to about $500. These systems include software for each user's workstation, which eliminates the need to set multiple switches required for simpler systems. Similar offerings and prices are available from some of the larger mail-order office and computer supply retailers as well.

Another method of sharing files and printers uses a data switch. Every desktop computer, printer, and modem to be linked is connected to a data switch via a cable from each device's serial port. The physical configuration resembles a star-shaped network, similar to most telephone systems.

Like a telephone system, a data switch establishes connections on demand and breaks them when a transmission is completed. Data switches were originally used to connect multiple dumb terminals to a large computer. Today, data switches also allow easy serial connections among IBM-compatible and Macintosh computers, as well as printers, modems, and other devices with serial ports.

Because the data switch's internal computer handles all the necessary processing and switching, data switches can carry information faster than the direct connections between computers made with products like LapLink discussed earlier. Although data switches are more expensive than such direct connections, they provide more LAN-like benefits, and for less money than most full-fledged LANs. Most data switch configurations cost under $150 per connection, less than the price of many network interface cards.

Most data switches are not as flexible as the typical fully configured advanced LAN. Data switches do not support as wide a combination of PCs, software, and media as most advanced LANs. Group computing solutions based on data switches can also be difficult to expand or to connect to other networks and resources. Nonetheless, their economy and simplicity make data switches appropriate alternatives for many work groups.

Using Multiuser Systems

Perhaps the most fully-featured LAN alternative is the multiuser system, one of those rare items in the computing world with a straightforward, descriptive name. A multiuser system is configured to allow multiple users to perform computing tasks simultaneously. Such a system offers solutions that are functionally similar to many LANs.

However, multiuser systems are implemented very differently from LANs. Some multiuser systems require a terminal on every user's desk, each connected to an expansion card located with others in a central chassis. Each card holds the equivalent of a PC's central microprocessor and some related chips, and the chassis contains the system memory and provides access to printers and other resources to be shared.

Functionally, this type of multiuser system can look very much like a LAN. Technologically, though, it's more like splitting your PC in half and putting one half in a cabinet down the hall, along with half of everybody else's PC. When more users are added to this type of system, it doesn't slow down as much as a LAN might with similar growth.

That's because everyone gets most of a PC to call their own, almost as if they were not connected at all.

Although they offer many LAN-like benefits, multiuser systems of this type are almost always less expensive than putting a full PC on everybody's desk and building a LAN. A popular and interesting example of such a system is PC-PLUS, from Alloy Computer. For its central cabinet and system host, PC-PLUS uses an IBM AT-class PC or compatible. When you want to add more users than there are expansion slots in the host, you can get add-on hardware from Alloy called PC-XBUS, which adds 12 slots and a power supply.

Instead of a network operating system, PC-PLUS comes with Network Executive software that works with the host computer's copy of DOS to provide the needed additional features. Alloy even offers a version of its Network Executive software that runs some versions of Novell's NetWare LAN operating system. For many organizations, this approach is an appropriate merging of the advantages of a LAN and a multiuser system. PC-PLUS managers can select from the same wealth of applications as managers of NetWare-based LANs, while enjoying the economies and performance levels of a multiuser system.

Another type of multiuser system uses powerful software to allow one powerful PC and other resources to be shared by several users, each equipped with either PCs or less expensive terminals. One popular example, Concurrent DOS 386, is from Digital Research, originators of the CP/M and DR-DOS products discussed earlier. As its name implies, Concurrent DOS 386 runs on systems based on the Intel 80386 chip and DOS, which include the most powerful IBM PCs and compatibles in widespread use today.

With Concurrent DOS 386 software and sufficient interfaces and system memory, a 80386-based PC can support simultaneous connections of several users' terminals. Release 3.0 of Concurrent DOS 386, introduced in late 1988, is priced at about $400 configured for up to 3 users and at about $500 configured for up to 10 users. In addition, the host system must be equipped with sufficient system memory and terminal interfaces for the maximum number of users supported. The latest version of Concurrent DOS 386 also supports direct transfer of files with LANs based on Novell's NetWare. Digital Research plans to provide greater compatibility with NetWare in future versions of Concurrent DOS 386.

Another popular variation of this kind of multiuser system is Multi-link Advanced, offered by a company called The Software Link. This product also allows an AT-class PC to support multiple users by combining efficient software with access to extra system memory and an expansion card for the AT that can support connection with up to eight terminals.

In addition, with sufficient extra system memory, up to eight users can each have the equivalent of an XT-class IBM-compatible PC, along with access to as much as 600,000 bytes of memory. (This is just a bit less than the maximum 640,000 bytes of system memory that a stand-alone XT can support.) All the leading applications that run on IBM-compatible LANs run under Multilink Advanced.

Multilink not only offers shared access to printers, storage, and modems, but it includes LAN-like features such as print queuing, an electronic bulletin board, and a variety of levels of user rights and privileges. In addition, several host PCs can themselves be connected with links similar to those that support each host's terminals. This optional LANLink feature permits the merging of several multiuser systems into something that's less expensive and slower than a true LAN, but that is functionally very similar to a LAN and that physically resembles the linked star networks described earlier.

*T*o LAN or Not to LAN?

There are numerous worthy alternatives to LANs, each with is particular strengths and weaknesses. There are also several key considerations that may make these alternatives to LANs worth considering for your work group.

Most LAN alternatives are simpler to install and maintain than most advanced LANs. If your group has few resources or personnel to devote to management of your work group solution, a LAN alternative may be a better choice.

Conversely, if your work group anticipates, or is experiencing, significant growth in size or computing requirements, you may be better off expending the extra effort and resources necessary to manage a LAN from the start. In such situations, your group will probably outgrow most LAN alternatives sooner or later. A true LAN is more likely to satisfy your long-term needs more effectively, despite the larger initial investment required. Only a well-executed needs and resource assessment can guide you adequately.

The skill level of your local reseller is also an important consideration when choosing between a LAN and a LAN alternative. Near-LANs are usually easier for resellers to support, just as they are easier for users to use and managers to manage. If you and your group now depend extensively on your reseller for support or training, you must take that reseller's expertise into account when choosing between a LAN and a near-LAN. If your reseller is not certified by the vendors of your preferred solution, you must agree on another solution, or another reseller.

Another consideration is whether your group is simply experimenting with work group solutions or committed to selecting and implementing a new solution. If you are experimenting, a near-LAN (or a simple, basic LAN) may make more sense, at least initially. However, should your experiment prove successful, the test solution may not have the power to remain in place, although it might be an ideal long-term solution for a particular subset of your work group or as a backup system during emergencies.

Many near-LAN solutions cannot support a mix of PC types easily, or at all. If your work group is already composed of users of multiple types of PCs, the only solution that embraces everyone may be a true LAN— or only the most sophisticated non-LAN, which can be just as difficult to implement and maintain as a true LAN.

Many network managers have discovered that diskless workstations, which are basically sophisticated terminals, can coexist well with full-fledged PCs on the same LANs. This integration requires careful matches between each user's requirements and the chosen desktop system.

In similar ways, LANs and near-LANs can often be integrated, as growing sophistication and computing needs dictate. This integration requires careful matches between currently available alternatives and current needs within and related to your group. In many cases, all but the most sophisticated near-LAN alternatives must be examined carefully to ensure that they support sufficient growth, enhancement, and interconnection with other solutions to avoid locking work group users and managers into solutions with no future.

Each LAN alternative must be evaluated as carefully as any LAN, because the differences between such alternatives may be more significant and less obvious than the differences between LAN offerings that are more popular and entrenched. However, LAN alternatives often have specific characteristics that provide specific benefits in specific situations. Careful needs assessment and evaluation of the market may yield an alternative that is not widely known, but is a better choice for your work group than a true LAN.

nine

9

Beyond Your LAN: Looking toward the Future

LANs are as important to your work group's future as they are to its present. Although the focus of most of this book has been on short-term concerns and solutions, this chapter looks at several issues that will affect you and your work group both in the near future and in the longer term. Considering such issues now will help ensure a work group computing solution that works now and is "futureproof" as well.

Your LAN and New Types of Servers

As discussed in Chapters 2 and 5, although most basic LANs and LAN alternatives can function without dedicated servers, advanced LANs require dedicated servers for the best performance and suite of available features. As networks get larger and user needs grow more complex, servers are becoming more important. The powers and functions supported by network servers are evolving as LANs themselves evolve into more powerful, client-server networks.

Today's Servers: Pluses and Minuses

Many of today's servers are not very different internally from the powerful PCs they serve. In fact, you can run some of the market's leading network server software on almost any sufficiently powerful IBM-compatible PC, which would need only more system memory, hard disk space, and network interface cards or ports to act as a server.

The use of regular PCs as servers is a straightforward and economical approach for many organizations' network requirements. Using regular PCs makes life easier for designers, builders, and sellers of servers as well. However, although such servers are easy to build, sell, and use without modification, they lack sufficient capacity to handle switching and processing of input and output from dozens or hundreds of network users. This limitation becomes a constraint as a network grows and as it uses applications that are larger and more complex.

Older, larger minicomputers and mainframes, in comparison, have more than enough of the input-output processing power that most PCs lack. However, most minicomputers and mainframes are designed to support terminals that communicate at relatively slow speeds rather than fully powered PCs that communicate at many megabits per second. Minicomputers and mainframes also don't run today's LAN operating systems easily. To make them do so would result in servers that were very complex, very expensive, and likely unreliable.

Among vendors of advanced LANs, Banyan and 3Com both have addressed this problem by developing and selling servers with some processing features not found in most equivalently powerful PCs. However, servers powerful enough for tomorrow's networks will go beyond these current solutions, incorporating designs and technology not found in today's servers.

The New Megaservers

In late 1989, a completely new server design was introduced by NetFrame Systems, Inc., of San Jose, California. NetFrame's principals spent five years developing a new architecture, which combines features from the worlds of mainframes, minicomputers, and desktop computers. In fact, the company refers to its servers as "network mainframes," a term that reflects their hybrid roots.

Each NetFrame server comes with a minimum of 380 megabytes of hard disk capacity and 8 megabytes of system memory. The most capacious version can have up to 6 gigabytes of disk storage space, and up to 64 megabytes of system memory. These capacities are greater than possible with any single server based on PC technology. In addition, NetFrame server capacity can be increased by the addition of expansion boards, rather than the addition of entire servers.

Each NetFrame server can use as its central processor an Intel 80386 or 80486 chip, the same types that drive the newest, most powerful PCs. Each NetFrame server also contains expansion cards, called I/O (for input/output) servers. Each of these cards also contains its own 80386-class chip, which does nothing but manage input and output. This multiple-processor approach allows NetFrame servers to perform at much higher speeds than can single-processor, PC-based servers, especially in larger networks. Both IBM-compatible and Apple Macintosh PCs can be served by NetFrame servers.

To move information around quickly, NetFrame's designers looked at how mainframes and minicomputers worked internally. They then had the relevant parts of these designs translated into custom-built processor chips. Such chips are called *ASICs*, for application-specific integrated circuits, and are used by many makers of computing hardware to improve the performance of their products. The chips inside each Net-Frame server, combined with multiple I/O processors and well-designed communications facilities, make the NetFrame products much more sophisticated than any server based on single-user PC technology alone.

NetFrame servers don't come with keyboards or screens, another departure from PC-based servers. However, NetFrame software that runs on any IBM-compatible PC on a network allows the user of that PC to manage multiple NetFrames servers. The ability to run this software from almost anywhere on the network and to manage multiple servers from a single point simplifies network management and administration, a boon for managers and users alike. NetFrame servers have extensive features that provide security, error correction, and reliability as well.

One of the most innovative NetFrame features is server-activated maintenance, or SAM. SAM automatically keeps log of all reported errors and saves all error information in RAM chips with their own batteries. Error information is therefore always available, a big help in isolating and correcting network problems. An historical record of problems is also valuable in predicting network growth and potential problem areas.

When a NetFrame server is set up, the network administrator can give NetFrame the telephone number that is usually called when network problems occur—typically the administrator's home or pager number. If a failure occurs, SAM will call the administrator and leave a number to call. The administrator can then learn the nature of the failure and, if necessary, even reconfigure or turn off a NetFrame server from a push-button tone telephone.

By including such features, the designers at NetFrame have made an important point and provided a useful benefit. The point is that as networks become larger and more important, they must become more reliable, or they lose their value to their users and organizations. The benefit is a powerful set of features to make networks more reliable and easier to fix.

Upon introduction of NetFrame's servers, Microsoft and Novell announced that they would adapt LAN Manager and NetWare 386 to run on the new systems, as did major vendors of database management software and other applications. NetFrame is developing new expansion boards, called application servers, that will allow databases and other resources to be manipulated easily and quickly on LANs that include NetFrame servers.

This response is an example of what may be the most important single feature of the NetFrame architecture, at least to LAN managers. The NetFrame servers, and those expected from other vendors, are designed for easy expansion of capacity and features, without the addition of multiple equipment cabinets. Just as file servers have come to include multiple disk drives and software for print service, the trend is toward each server providing multiple services.

Having one server provide multiple services increases network performance and reliability by reducing the number and size of critical network components. It also increases networks' flexibility and responsiveness to users' needs by making the addition of features and capacity faster and less expensive. The NetFrame servers represent a giant step toward full realization of this trend and its benefits to LAN users and managers.

Shortly after NetFrame's servers were introduced, Compaq Computer Corporation announced new systems that have the potential to become megaservers as well. The Compaq Systempro offers capacious system memory and hard-disk storage space and supports multiple 80386 or 80486 chips as well. Although architecturally different from NetFrame's servers and touted by Compaq primarily as a replacement for advanced workstations, the Systempro also has a future as a network megaserver. Leading network software vendors are supporting the Systempro as enthusiastically as they are supporting NetFrame's servers.

When competing market leaders support the same new products, those products clearly are important and likely have a long, prosperous life ahead. The features of the NetFrame servers and Compaq Systempro are not just interesting or of value only to LAN managers. Users can expect to see changes in their LANs as features like those in these systems become more common. Such features make shared computing resources more accessible and dependable—benefits to every LAN user.

Communications and Databases: Coming Soon to Servers on Your Network

The systems described in the preceding section are examples of an emerging new generation of network servers. Other types of servers also are appearing, to bring still greater abilities and performance levels to networks like yours. Two of the most interesting new types of servers are communications servers and database servers, mentioned in Chapter 2.

File servers manage access to files, and print servers manage access to printers. In much the same way, communications servers manage a PC's access to a variety of communications methods and facilities, and database servers distribute information requests to an organization's information storage facilities and return the information requested. The following sections present a brief look at what's here now and what's coming.

Communications Servers: Extending Your PC's Reach

If you've ever seen a meeting of the General Assembly at the United Nations, you've no doubt been impressed by the facilities for listening to speakers. A member can sit in any seat, put on the headphones plugged into it, and listen to the proceedings in any of a number of languages.

The wiring for the entire meeting area is connected to a central site elsewhere, where a room full of interpreters act collectively as a communications server. They provide near-immediate delivery of the information being shared, transparently translated into formats best used by everyone "on the network." This example demonstrates some of the benefits communications servers can bring to LANs.

Soon after you and your colleagues are connected via a LAN, some of you are going to need the ability to communicate with another work group, another site of your organization, a larger computer at some other site, a distant electronic information network, or all of the preceding.

For example, in many organizations, one of the main benefits of LANs is the ease of communications between desktop PCs and the organization's mainframes and minicomputers. These larger systems and external networks almost always contain information that work groups need to use, and LANs can help make that task easier.

For a system like that of the United Nations, each listener's headphones must have access to all available languages. Otherwise, each seat would need a separate set of headphones for each available language, which wouldn't leave much room to sit. Similarly, if you had to have a separate workstation on your desk for access to every computing resource available to you, you'd have no room to work. Instead, you are connected to a LAN, and your PC connects you to all the resources of the LAN.

To be connected to other external resources like those mentioned in the preceding paragraphs, however, most LANs need a separate bridge, gateway, or router for each type of connection between the LAN and the other resources, including other LANs. Numerous computing vendors market such products. Many of these products are evolving to support wider varieties of connections and to become more versatile communications servers.

For example, Digital Equipment Corporation markets a system called PCLAN/Server, which can connect hundreds of DOS- and OS/2-based PCs to DEC minicomputers. Hewlett-Packard's analagous offering, HP Network Services LAN Gateway, links NetWare LANs to HP minicomputers. This software runs on a system compatible to an IBM PC-AT and supports up to 30 users. Both DEC and HP are working to build more and better links between their own systems and those of other vendors, thus expanding the resources available through PCs to LAN users connected to PCLAN/Server or HP Gateway.

Alantec of Fremont, California, markets a range of products that provide LAN-to-LAN connections. Alantec Multi-LAN Switch, or MLS, links up to 16 separate Ethernet-based LANs. These LANs can then be used and managed as if they were one network, even if the separate LANs use different types of communications cable and operate at different speeds.

Late in 1989, Microsoft and Digital Communications Associates began shipping a new software product called (unambiguously enough) Communications Server. This product is designed to run in concert with Microsoft's LAN Manager software, discussed in Chapter 6. Communications Server provides easy linkage between LANs operating with LAN Manager and networks of larger computers operating with Systems Network Architecture (or SNA). SNA was created more than 20 years ago by IBM as a standard method for connecting its larger systems. SNA is a foundation of most of today's networks of IBM and compatible minicomputers and mainframes, old and new.

With LAN Manager and Communications Server, IBM-compatible PCs running DOS or OS/2 can communicate directly with almost any large IBM-compatible computer and can do anything a terminal connected to that computer can usually do. After performing tasks using the software resources of the larger computer, the PC user can insert the results into a spreadsheet, local database, document, or whatever other application requires them.

Eventually, Communications Server will provide similarly transparent linkage to a broad range of computers, networks, and databases. This linkage will allow desktop workstations based on DOS, OS/2, UNIX, and perhaps even the Macintosh operating system to communicate easily with SNA-linked networks of mainframes and minicomputers and the information resources they contain.

In the near future, communications servers will combine the functions of products like these. Just as a file server makes file sharing easier, communications servers will make connections beyond your LAN easier to build and use. Other vendors are already developing such products in recognition of their obvious benefits to LAN users.

Database Servers: What You Get Is What You Need

You're sitting at your PC creating a report. The report includes information from several of your organization's databases, located within computers scattered throughout the enterprise. Nonetheless, you're able to get the results you want through simple queries, without regard for which information resides where.

Database servers can make such a scenario reality. Database servers are software designed to run in concert with network software on a physical server, like some print servers and the Communications Server product from DCA and Microsoft. When you enter a query at your PC, database server software, which has been told about all the databases available to you, performs the processing necessary to deliver the results you desire. What you get is what you need.

Several database servers now exist that let you and your colleagues use your PCs and database software to take at least some advantage of the greater database processing power of minicomputers and mainframes. Their features are worth a brief look as indicators of what's likely coming to your LAN.

(You don't need to know how these products work to understand their importance, though you do need to know about SQL, or structured query language. SQL is a widely accepted, standard set of rules that let database applications communicate with databases and with each other. It is supported by every major vendor of database software and database servers. You also need to know that database servers are designed to work with LANs based on OS/2, and not the older and less powerful DOS. However, DOS-based PCs can usually be employed as work-stations on such LANs with minimal difficulty.)

Microsoft has thrown its considerable influence behind a product called SQL Server. A companion product called DB-Library allows applications developed by others to communicate with SQL Server easily, and invisibly to users of the applications. SQL Server already works with the dBASE product line, sold by Ashton-Tate. Programs written in the dBASE programming language need no modification to work with SQL Server, save for the addition of commands directed at SQL, if desired.

SQL Server is also directly compatible with Sybase products, which manipulate databases on a wide variety of systems. As with DOS and OS/2, most other leading software vendors will likely make their applications work with this Microsoft offering.

If you are using or planning an OS/2-based LAN and you have database requirements, you'd do well to begin anticipating your database server needs now. At the very least, you should select desktop database applications that are compatible with SQL Server. Expect to see large numbers of SQL Server–supported systems appear rapidly during the early 1990s.

Companies known primarily for database solutions have also begun to develop and market database servers, with their previous flagship products as foundations. Oracle Corporation, of Belmont, California, is currently the largest supplier of database software in the world, with integrated products that run on everything from independent desktop PCs to LANs and supercomputers, systems smaller and far more powerful than multiple mainframes.

In 1989, Oracle announced a plan to introduce database servers for NetWare 386, OS/2, UNIX, and Banyan's VINES environments, to allow easy access to databases managed by Oracle software from any of these environments. Oracle Server for NetWare 386 makes the Oracle server available to users of NetFrame computers, which run NetWare 386. Application developers can write or adapt their products to work with the Oracle servers and deliver to PC users information processed by any computers running Oracle software on those users' networks.

All Oracle products use SQL and are available for use on PCs, mini-computers, and mainframes. Barring unforeseeable circumstances, users and applications developers can depend on Oracle to keep its networks and database software products current and tightly integrated. These are important features to those investing in the future of client-server computing.

In looking toward the future, however, it's important not to forget the past. In that spirit, Gupta Technologies of Menlo Park, California, developed SQLBase. This database server is different from Oracle's in that it operates under DOS and does not require OS/2 to perform multiple tasks seemingly simultaneously, although it runs faster under OS/2.

In fact, SQLBase performs multiple tasks near simultaneously. The software accepts multiple user requests, divides them into tasks, and then schedules their execution quickly, but one at a time.

Lotus Development, owners of a part of database company Sybase, reportedly plans to use Gupta's technology as the foundation for a product called Lotus/DBMS (for Lotus Database Management System). Even without that product, the ability of Gupta's server to operate with DOS or OS/2 makes it unique among this emerging class of products.

*N*ew Servers + New Services = Client-Server Computing

If you combine the benefits of the new types of servers with better LANs, you begin to see a clearer picture of true client-server computing. To better understand client-server computing, think for a moment about electronic mail. When you use e-mail, your PC does part of the work, such as providing facilities that let you read, create, and edit messages. However, another, larger computer somewhere else does part of the work, too, such as routing and delivering your messages.

Electronic mail is an example of a distributed application. The ability to handle such an application is what sets client-server computing apart from most of today's LANs. In a true client-server network, many applications are distributed among the many servers (including applications servers like those being planned by NetFrame and others), so that each computer does what it does best for every network user. Distributed applications, like those made possible by the database servers described in the preceding section, will proliferate, as will other tools for transparent, dynamic information sharing and provision of network and computing services.

Your LAN and the New PCs

While change roils the network waters around you and your colleagues, other changes are affecting your very desktop. Because your PC is your window onto your network, these changes bear some scrutiny on your part. This information will help you understand the issues attracting attention in the computing press and determine which are important to your organization.

PCs and DOS, PS/2s and OS/2: Features and Differences

Soon after the introduction of the 80386 chip, IBM, the leader of the market, began shipping a new generation of PCs, which IBM dubbed the PS/2 family (for personal system/2). All but the least powerful of these are designed to run OS/2, the operating system written to take advantage of the 80386 that powers them.

However, the differences between PS/2s and OS/2 make them and the programs they run sometimes incompatible with systems compatible with older IBM PCs, XTs, and ATs. This means that IBM now sells PCs incompatible with its own older products. Thus, before alternatives such as Macintosh computers or other workstations can even be considered, users and managers must sort out the differences among IBM and IBM-compatible PCs old and new and see if these differences matter.

The Good News

PS/2 and OS/2 systems are more powerful and more compatible with the rest of IBM's computing network strategies than are older PCs and compatibles based on DOS. These strategies encompass the larger IBM systems used by many organizations that also use IBM-compatible PCs independently and on LANs.

Also, OS/2 includes features, such as Microsoft Windows and Presentation Manager, not found in DOS. These features make what you see on your screen more graphical (or based on pictures instead of words) and easier to understand than the typical A> or C> prompt that DOS displays. Windows lets you divide your PC screen into multiple active areas, which each can run a different application. Presentation Manager provides a consistent graphical interface between you and all your PC applications.

Also, OS/2 supports Microsoft's LAN Manager, discussed in Chapter 6. Although this feature is more relevant to your LAN servers than to your desktop PC, the ability of OS/2 to support LAN Manager is a key distinction between OS/2 and DOS. Whether or not your servers run OS/2 and LAN Manager directly affects the network features available on your desktop. A desktop PC based on OS/2 can more easily take advantage of many advanced features and applications than can DOS-based PCs connected to OS/2-based servers.

The Not-So-Good News

However, these distinctions between the new and the old may not make sufficient difference to convince you and your work group to trade your DOS-based PCs for PS/2 systems. For users, the new PCs mean getting used to new ways of working, with icons (or pictures) instead of file or program names and a Macintosh-like mouse (or hand-held pointing device) in addition to a regular keyboard. Even familiar applications can look and act very different when transported from DOS to OS/2.

Another important consideration is cost. The new PCs are much more expensive than the old PCs. And although the older systems can't run OS/2, they can run all the applications you and your colleagues use now. In addition, a sufficiently powerful older machine and hard disk drive is just as fast as a PS/2 system with many of these applications.

As is true so often with DOS-based PCs, the purchase price of a system is just the beginning of its true cost. Most DOS-based machines now come equipped with 640,000 bytes of system memory, the maximum DOS can manage. Some can be equipped with extra memory, which DOS can be tricked into using, but most perform adequately as user workstations with 640K (and perhaps a bit more to be used as a RAM disk, or very fast imitation of an additional disk drive).

In comparison, most OS/2-based machines need at least one megabyte, or a million bytes, of system memory, and they really need several megabytes to provide maximum benefit to their users. With a megabyte of memory currently priced anywhere between $400 and $800, depending on source and worldwide chip market conditions, prices for OS/2-based workstations can climb quickly.

Similar conditions hold for hard disk drives, which are options with DOS and requirements with OS/2. The newer, faster, more capacious disk drives (and their controlling circuit boards) designed for the new PCs are more expensive than their older, slower counterparts used with most DOS-based systems. The video monitors and controllers for the new PCs are more expensive as well, because they must be of sufficient quality to display the graphics of OS/2, Windows, and Presentation Manager.

If you turn to an OS/2-based system, your older PC's expansion cards will likely need replacing as well. The newer PCs use an entirely new method for communicating with such cards, which IBM calls microchannel architecture, or MCA. New network interface adapters that support MCA are available now, and they are more expensive than those that are not MCA compatible.

(Some manufacturers of IBM-compatible PCs have banded together to build PCs that run OS/2 but allow use of current expansion cards. This architecture is called extended industry standard architecture, and its supporters are referred to as the EISA group. However, members of this group have announced that EISA-compatible machines may not appear until 1992 or 1993. Some major manufacturers will likely market MCA-compatible and EISA-compatible systems, increasing the number of options you must consider.)

Overall, the price difference between 80386-based systems and older IBM-compatible PCs can range from a few hundred to several thousand dollars. The higher cost may make needed PC enhancements such as extra system memory more difficult for your work group to afford. In fact, the combined trends of rising prices and increased use of graphics and pointing devices are already enough to make many users of IBM-compatible PCs consider a Macintosh as an alternative.

The Best News

Although PCs based on the 80386 chip and OS/2 operating system may be more powerful and expensive *workstations* than many users need or want, such systems make wonderfully powerful, cost-effective LAN *servers*. Currently, few standalone applications take full advantage of the power of the new chip and operating system combination. However, faster servers and new network services can readily justify the extra power and expense.

Network applications are easier to create under OS/2 than under DOS and offer new and potentially potent revenue sources for their developers. This is why there are so many new network operating systems, database servers, and other products that take advantage of the power of the new 80386 and OS/2 platforms.

Many standalone OS/2 applications, meanwhile, are still just slightly enhanced versions of their DOS-based predecessors and not really new applications with new powers. This is evidence that developers believe many of us are going to keep our DOS-based IBM-compatible PCs for some time to come, and that those developers intend to keep providing software for these systems.

Some software companies have not only refused to abandon the older PCs, but continue to enhance their offerings for these systems, sometimes while developing new programs for the new PCs as well. Quarterdeck Office Systems of Santa Monica, California, with its DESQview product family, offers perhaps the best-known example of this strategy.

Quarterdeck's DESQview brings true a multitasking environment; a consistent, clear interface; easy transfer of information among applications; and other features to DOS-based software. DESQview 386, meanwhile, helps users manage the running of multiple DOS and OS/2 tasks, and the exchange of information among them, on the same 80386-based PC. Quarterdeck also markets software tools to applications developers to help these developers easily incorporate DESQview's advantages into their own products.

Other companies also continue to develop innovative improvements for the older PCs. Most notable among these is Borland International, developers of the SideKick pop-up desk accessories. Borland's Quattro spreadsheet offers features and performance that compare favorably to those of the Lotus 1-2-3 spreadsheet. However, whereas version 3.0 of

1-2-3 requires at least 1 megabyte of system memory, Quattro works within the 640K available to XT-class IBM-compatible PCs.

(Borland's technology is called VROOMM, for virtual real-time object-oriented memory management. VROOMM divides software into small chunks and swaps these chunks in and out of system memory as they are needed. This method allows very large and complex programs to run efficiently on systems that can't manage large amounts of system memory.)

What does all this mean to you? When choosing among IBM-compatible workstations, especially if budgets are tight, make sure you have very solid reasons before switching to a PS/2 and OS/2 system. If your work group does not use at least one application that must run under OS/2, the switch may cost you more in time and frustration, and your organization more in money, than any benefits warrant.

PCs based on DOS and 80286-class or older chips are much less expensive and better understood by users, managers, vendors, and repair providers. A wealth of proven software is available for these machines, and they can tap into additional power as needed via LANs and 80386-based servers.

If you and your colleagues are happy with your current PCs and application, then select computing network solutions that let you keep these elements. If you're not happy, try to upgrade what you have before replacing it with the most current technology. You may be able to increase your PC's system memory, hard disk drive speed or capacity, or overall performance with enhancements less expensive than a new, state-of-the-art PC.

*W*hat Does the Macintosh Mean to Your LAN?

In the desktop computing marketplace, Apple Computer's Macintosh computer family has rapidly moved from office curiosity to a worthy alternative to DOS-based desktop systems. The evolution of Macintosh computers definitely affects your LAN if you or any colleagues use or plan to use a Macintosh system. Macintosh technology also affects your desktop system, even if you are not a Macintosh user.

Unlike DOS-based systems, Macintosh PCs can easily integrate text and graphics both on screen and on paper. In addition, Macintosh computers rely on graphics to present information to users. Instead of having to remember strings of words and characters, as is often required with DOS-based PCs, Macintosh users simply "point" at pictures representing files or programs and press a button on a mouse to move information around, to launch (or start) applications, and to invoke commands.

These features let even novice PC users easily perform relatively complex tasks, such as constructing and editing documents with text and pictures. The consistency of the Macintosh graphical interface from application to application also makes Macintosh computers easy to use.

The earliest Macintosh computers were viewed as underpowered toys by managers and software developers focused on the business computing marketplace of the mid 1980s. Then came desktop publishing: an application with value to businesses that DOS-based PCs couldn't support.

Soon, Apple and Macintosh supporters found and created other niches where the new computer with the radical design had important impact. Its graphical nature had its most profound effect on business users in areas related to word processing and document creation. In the space of months, Macintosh computers caused business people to look at traditional applications in different ways.

Meanwhile, as the number LANs dominated by IBM-compatible PCs grew, so did the number of Macintosh enthusiasts clamoring for equal access to computing resources. Positive response came grudgingly at first, as users and managers of IBM-compatible PCs and LANs still viewed the Macintosh with some disdain. Developers familiar with the IBM-compatible PC environment also took longer than they and hopeful users expected to adapt their existing products and develop new ones.

In response, Apple (and other developers of hardware and software) continued to improve the Macintosh and its ability to work in environments dominated by IBM-compatible PCs. Business applications began to appear that were not only as powerful as their IBM-compatible equivalents, but shared information easily with them. This made Macintosh computers much more readily acceptable as working partners for users and managers of IBM-compatible LANs.

For many individuals and organizations, the longest-standing objection to the Macintosh was its expense relative to an IBM-compatible PC with a similar set of features. However, as discussed previously, IBM compatibles are getting more expensive as they become more powerful. This trend, plus continued enhancements to the Macintosh that aren't easily duplicated in DOS-based PCs, are breaking down this last important barrier to the Macintosh's serious acceptance by what is basically an IBM-compatible world of PCs and LANs.

The Macintosh is now taken seriously by most as a business tool in its own right. The product line continues to grow in power and flexibility and is now available in a range of portable and desktop configurations. Newer, more powerful Macintosh computers rival high-end PS/2-compatible PCs and many UNIX-based advanced workstations in their performance. Newer Macintosh computers even resemble IBM-compatible PCs physically, with expansion slots in their system units and optional, IBM-like expanded keyboards available as options.

Products also are available that allow Macintosh computers to run some DOS-based applications. However, in most cases a separate DOS-based PC is a less expensive and simpler solution than enhancing a Macintosh to support DOS.

Will Macintosh and IBM-compatible PCs ever be directly, totally compatible? Not as long as they are based on fundamentally different technologies, and Apple continues to treat its chosen technology as closed. However, as LANs evolve into true client-server networks, Macintosh computers and DOS-based PCs will gain equal access to the same applications and to other connected computing resources.

A Macintosh is very different from a DOS-based PC when the two are independent, but on a client-server network, a client is a client. In such an environment, those who like the Macintosh can use it, and those familiar with DOS-based PCs can use them, with or without OS/2, Windows, or Presentation Manager.

Meanwhile, the Macintosh computer line is well worth watching as a harbinger of new classes of applications for Macintosh and DOS-based PCs alike. The benefits of hypermedia and hyperinformation, or diverse images and information that can be easily and dynamically linked, were first delivered to business computing users on the Macintosh and are now moving onto IBM-compatible PCs. HyperPAD, from Brightbill-Roberts of Syracuse, New York, combines a visual interface, Hyper-Card-like information management, and easy development of custom applications for users of DOS-based PCs.

Desktop media, the combination of audio, video, and text-based information into new types of presentations, is another application emerging in the DOS world, but pioneered on Macintosh platforms. Therefore, even if your work group never uses one, the Macintosh computer is worth your attention, especially as your LAN and your needs evolve.

*A*dvanced Workstations and the Specter of UNIX

Along with Macintosh PCs, advanced workstations are beginning to appear in more and more LANs. These powerful, fast, and highly graphical systems, not to be confused with the diskless workstations discussed in Chapter 1, have important strengths and shortcoming and, like the Macintosh, are evolving in ways that are of interest and potential importance to all LAN users.

Advanced workstations were originally designed for applications far more complex and dependent on high-quality graphics than word processing or even desktop publishing. These workstations were intended for use by engineers who design engines or buildings, by scientists who create and manipulate models of complex compounds, and by others with similarly complex needs. Workstations from suppliers (such as Hewlett-Packard; IBM; and Sun Microsystems, makers of the TOPS LAN products) are still used primarily for such types of applications.

To meet these requirements, workstations need powerful internal computing power and the ability to display high-resolution graphics, often in multiple colors. To allow users to examine objects on their screens from different perspectives, workstations must be able to update displayed information quickly and smoothly enough to make displayed objects look like real objects being turned.

Like today's business workers, engineers and designers usually work on specific projects in small groups, with frequent need to interact with other groups and individuals. Workstations therefore have a long history of being connected in networks, both to each other and to databases residing on minicomputers or mainframes.

With their features, advanced workstations seem to combine the best features of powerful PCs and computing networks. They tend to be based on chips much more powerful than those that power PCs and to be able to manage far more system memory and larger hard disk drives than can typical PCs. When combined with high-powered servers, advanced workstations are powerful work group solutions indeed.

However, advanced workstations have a history of limited success among business work groups. Early advanced workstations were far more expensive than terminals and the first PCs. Also, few applications, such as word processing applications, were straightforward enough for business people to use effectively. Because most advanced workstation users come from backgrounds that include computing and science or engineering, they are more comfortable than most business people in working with software far more powerful than it is friendly and easy to learn.

Business people require applications they can understand and use effectively without technical backgrounds. From their beginnings, PCs and the applications they support have been aimed directly at such people and have been easier to afford and to use effectively than advanced workstations. The advantages workstations offer to their primary, more technical users do not outweigh their problems to potential business users.

However, some workstation vendors are now making efforts to become better friends with business users (and buyers). As PCs become more sophisticated and expensive, workstation makers are introducing entry-level offerings at prices competitive with those of the new PCs. Sun Microsystems' SPARCstation I retails at prices beginning at about $9,000 and outperforms many high-end IBM-compatible and Macintosh PCs. Digital Equipment Corporation offers several aggressively priced advanced workstations as well.

In addition, more business-savvy applications, including some adapted versions of programs familiar to DOS users, are becoming available. Also, some workstation members are adding to their offerings the ability to participate in LANs based on operating systems popular in the business world. Such network participation makes the direct incompatibilities between workstations and office PCs less important, as it does with the incompatibilities between IBM-compatible PCs and Macintosh computers.

What's NeXT in Workstations?

Perhaps the most relevant example of the advanced workstation's evolution is the NeXT system, which is offered by a company founded by Apple co-founder Steven Jobs. Originally intended for users in the academic market only, the NeXT system is now available commercially and has a combination of features unmatched by most desktop computing systems.

Each NeXT system combines a 17-inch high-resolution monitor, a superb audio system, and hard disk drives that can hold hundreds of megabytes. NeXT laser printers produce output at 400 dots per inch, compared to 300 dots per inch for such printers as the HP LaserJet. The NeXT "floppy" drive is actually an optical disk drive, which reads and writes information with lasers.

The NeXT system also comes with a full suite of software applications and useful tools. Chief among these is an integrated set of writing tools on optical disk, including the *Oxford Complete Works of William Shakespeare,* the *Oxford Dictionary of Quotations,* and *Merriam-Webster's Collegiate Dictionary and Thesaurus.* The system's technical documentation is also supplied on optical disk.

Applications include a version of the Macintosh world's Write Now word processor, Sybase's SQL database server, and NeXT Electronic Mail with voice mail features. The system also comes with software that helps users create and manage memos, messages, reminders, and other documents. Mathematica, a tool for advanced mathematical calculations, and a version of the programming language called LISP round out the software included with each NeXT computer. LISP is widely used by programmers who work under the UNIX operating system.

The NeXT operating system is called Mach and is a powerful, graphical, multitasking derivation of UNIX. It uses icons, or pictures, to represent documents and programs in a fashion similar to, but different from, the Macintosh, Microsoft Windows, and Presentation Manager. IBM was so impressed with the NeXT user interface that it licensed the rights to use the same interface with its own version of UNIX, which IBM calls AIX.

With all this, perhaps the most impressive feature is the price of the system. The basic system currently sells for just under $10,000, which is a very aggressive price for such computing power and more than competitive with high-end Macintosh and PS/2-class PCs. More than 70 developers of DOS-, OS/2-, and Macintosh-based software, including Novell and Oracle, have or are developing NeXT-compatible applications.

The NeXT system has some characteristics that may be perceived as shortcomings by some users. For example, the system is so far available only with monochrome (noncolor) displays. However, the NeXT system's impressive combination of features and price will likely convince more software developers to support it, and more LAN users and managers to consider it.

Sun Microsystems, a leading vendor of more traditional advanced workstations, also has a line of lower-priced, high-performance systems designed to compete with high-end PCs. These are called SPARCstations and are based on special chips developed by Sun and adopted by other computing manufacturers.

NeXT, Sun, and other vendors of advanced workstations will continue to make their offerings more affordable and more compatible with traditional LAN environments, as user workstations or as servers. Users and managers are advised to keep an eye on these vendors and their forthcoming offerings.

Your LAN and UNIX

Most workstations and many nonbusiness networks depend on the UNIX operating system, so the potential impact of UNIX on your LAN is worth your consideration. First, a bit of information about UNIX itself is in order.

UNIX is a very powerful operating system with simultaneous support of multiple users and multiple tasks built in rather than added on as it is with DOS. UNIX has also been around for a long time and is well understood by workstation makers, software developers, and many nonbusiness users, particularly in academia.

UNIX has other features that make it a worthy competitor to OS/2. Among these is the ability to get files from and send files to any connected devices, whether screens, disk or tape drives, or printers (for output only, of course). UNIX also lets programmers easily send output from one computing task as input to another task, allowing easy interoperation of properly written applications. In addition, UNIX is structured so that it looks and acts the same on mainframes, minicomputers, and desktop systems, a feature that facilitates software development and use.

UNIX, like OS/2, offers some potentially major benefits to users of desktop computers and LANs. However, like OS/2, UNIX is not without its drawbacks. One of the most obvious of these is the typical UNIX user interface. Without an intermediary shell program, UNIX is definitely unfriendly to users and programmers alike. (DOS and OS/2 also suffer from unfriendliness, which is why shells such as DesqView and Presentation Manager are so popular.)

Historically, the most important drawback of UNIX has been the lack of industry agreement on a single version of the operating system. However, AT&T, the first marketers of UNIX, has made technological and political moves to spur consolidation. AT&T's UNIX System V now incorporates features of BSD UNIX, derived from AT&T's version by software engineers at the University of California at Berkeley; Xenix, the version of UNIX for PCs marketed by Microsoft; and SCO UNIX from the Santa Cruz Operation in California.

Although there is now some consensus on the operating system itself, there is still conflict over what UNIX-based applications should look like. Much of academia and some commercial developers have endorsed X/Window, the user interface designed at the Massachusetts Institute of Technology (MIT). AT&T is promoting its own interface, known as Open Look. Meanwhile, the Open Software Foundation (OSF), a consortium of UNIX vendors, has developed its own interface, called Motif.

Motif strongly resembles Presentation Manager, the user interface deemed the standard of the future for IBM-compatible PCs by Microsoft and IBM. In preparation for integrating their economies during the 1990s, the European Community has given a coalition called the European Commission responsibility for integrating UNIX-based computing solutions. The commission has chosen Motif as its designated user interface, in part because there is still no broad-based support for Open Look or other contenders in the United States.

While the process of industry consolidation behind a dominant version of UNIX and user interface continues, the range of available applications will be limited. Developers simply can't afford to write several slightly different versions of each UNIX product and will therefore continue to focus their attention on DOS and OS/2 until even more consensus exists among UNIX supporters.

Needless to say, AT&T continues to promote UNIX-based systems as ideal for work group computing. However, like the 80386 chip and OS/2, the best place for UNIX may be in your LAN's servers, and not on your desktop. UNIX workstations are more expensive than many PCs, and using UNIX-based PCs means getting and learning new applications before you can do your work.

When a network is based on UNIX servers, PCs running MS-DOS, OS/2, or UNIX can all be used as clients. A UNIX-based server can also support communications and database services, as can a sufficiently powerful server based on OS/2. AT&T servers can also run DOS applications that run from a server (instead of residing entirely at a workstation) through software AT&T calls Simul-Task/386.

Thus, although UNIX may not now be cost effective for desktop PCs, it can nevertheless provide some real benefits to your LAN servers without introducing unfamiliar features at user workstations. (In this regard, UNIX is similar to Banyan's VINES network operating system, discussed in Chapter 6.)

In the short term, though, UNIX is important only to the extent that your chosen LAN solution providers support it. If UNIX is implemented properly in your LAN, you should never even see it. If UNIX is implemented properly across the industry, you shouldn't have to pay attention to it until long after the numerous confusions and conflicts are resolved by the various government, academic, technical, and software development forces driving the UNIX marketplace.

Your LAN and ISDN

A term you, your colleagues, and managers are likely to hear a lot about during the next few years is integrated services digital network, or ISDN. ISDN technology has been fraught with confusion, misinterpretation, and overstatement since its inception. Although it may have little direct effect on your LAN and how it works, you should know something about ISDN.

ISDN is really little more than a new way of connecting devices into networks. It's a set of technological recommendations that, when fully implemented, allow a single telephone line to carry multiple digital transmissions as well as information sufficient to manage them and keep them separate. These transmissions can be voice calls, computer communications, facsimiles, graphics, or other data that can be stored and transmitted digitally.

As you can imagine, a world wired for ISDN would facilitate all types of communications, including that among work groups. You could plug telephone-type lines into the back of your ISDN-compatible PC and contact a colleague's computer as easily as you make a call on your telephone system. In addition, you could communicate with a colleague across the continent as easily as with one in your building.

In short, if ISDN were adopted and implemented uniformly by all suppliers of network services (including the local and long-distance telephone companies) and telecommunications and computing products, it would provide a uniform set of pathways for efficient digital communications, as ubiquitous and easy to use as today's modern telephone networks.

ISDN's resemblance to a telephone network is no coincidence. ISDN's strongest promoters are, in fact, providers of telecommunication services, particularly AT&T. The reasons for this are straightforward, although not necessarily obvious. While digital communication needs, like those spurred by the desire for work group computing solutions, are growing rapidly, the demand for plain old telephone service, or POTS, as it's called, is growing slowly. To participate in the growth of digital communications, telephone companies must be able to provide digital pathways, and not just the older, analog circuits that still carry many voice transmissions.

Telephone networks already reach almost every place on the planet, and almost every business already has telephone systems in place. A digital upgrade and expansion of the network that already connects these systems and their users could offer great advantages to users and providers at minimal cost. Telephone companies could provide newer and more competitive communications services, based on a network already familiar to its users.

ISDN has therefore been touted by many as *the* solution to future communications needs, including those of LAN users. For example, ISDN is a potentially powerful medium for linking LANs with other LANs as well as with other computing and communications resources. Alas, as with any near-Utopia, many obstacles and unresolved issues stand between today's situation and widely available ISDN-based services.

Much of what is unresolved about ISDN concerns when and where it will be available and what form it will take. Two types of ISDN exist: basic rate and primary rate. Primary rate is full-blown ISDN, but is more expensive to implement than the lower-capacity basic rate.

Implementation choices of type and timing will be made by network service providers based on demonstrated and perceived demand.

However, there won't likely be any great demand from users until there are more real-life implementations and applications potential users can evaluate. Some of these exist today, but they are limited in number and in scope.

Even in areas where ISDN circuits are already available, they are not equally available to all. This is because telephone companies must have switching computers in their central offices that are more sophisticated and expensive than those installed in many locations. An urban area with many corporate customers will likely have widespread access to ISDN-based services sooner than rural areas. Thus, some corporations may not be able to include remote sites in their ISDN for some time after such networks are built.

The world's telecommunications providers are attempting to agree on ways to implement ISDN across local, regional, and national boundaries. However, the lack of proven user demand and the ever-changing face of the regulations governing United States telecommunications will continue to limit availability of ISDN services for at least the short term.

Communications equipment that is ISDN compatible is becoming more commonplace, but little ISDN-based communications or computing has filtered down to the LAN user's desktop yet. In the short term, the most important computing applications for ISDN will be links between large computers and user terminals or between larger computers and LANs.

If you are a member of a network that communicates extensively with outside resources via modem, you are more likely to confront ISDN sooner than if you are not. Several companies are now developing or marketing ISDN-based equipment for linking separate networks. Systems now being marketed by companies such as Aria Communications (San Francisco, California) and DCA (Alpharetta, Georgia) combine shared access to ISDN channels with innovative support of network management and other features.

Nonetheless, in the short term, ISDN will be more of a curiosity than a concern to LAN users and of limited interest to most LAN managers. Knowledge of the current state of affairs is still of value, though, to protect you from being lured into a technology before its time, or yours.

Your LAN and Industry Standards

As the previous discussions of issues—from multivendor LANs to ISDN—indicate, the role of standards is wide ranging and very important to you and your LAN in both the short and long terms. As discussed briefly in Chapter 3, true industry standards continue to emerge and evolve, helping pave an increasingly smoother road to interoperability: the easy sharing of all computing resources by all network users, regardless of the source or location of those resources.

In the short term, standards can provide useful product selection guidelines for LAN users and managers. Standards can help provide users with consistent, predictable access to network features, even as those features change. Standards help managers build more future-proof networks, by providing smooth links between today's and tomorrow's solutions.

As you've no doubt noticed, standards are proliferating in almost every area of computing and communications. New technologies continue to beget new standards, even as more mature standards become more entrenched. Meanwhile, standards bodies such as the International Standards Organization (ISO) and the American National Standards Institute (ANSI) continue to promote open, or vendor-independent, standards, while leading vendors promote their own solutions as de facto standards.

Of all the standards that exist or are emerging, only a few are really important to LAN users in the short term. Some of these affect how information travels around your LAN, and some affect how information is presented on your PC screen.

Ethernet–Twisted-Pair Transmission Standards

One of the most interesting emerging LAN-related standards is called 10-base-T. This oddly named standard gives product makers a set of rules for carrying Ethernet transmissions over twisted-pair cable instead of over the more expensive coaxial cable used in most Ethernet-based LANs.

Although several current products now allow the combination of Ethernet and twisted-pair cable, none is based on a true industry standard. Under the guidance of the IEEE, the 10-base-T recommendations are due to become that standard. This standard also is likely to be adopted by all major LAN vendors sooner or later.

Once initial development of the 10-base-T standard is completed, product makers will be able to incorporate its rules and instructions into their offerings, as software or on chips. Intel Corporation is developing a set of chips that will make many LAN products compatible with 10-base-T.

Users of products without modular, future-proof designs may have to replace instead of upgrade their systems. You and your managers thus should keep the progress of 10-base-t in mind when purchasing Ethernet LAN components. You should also give preference to those products that allow easy upgrading as the standard evolves.

Fiber-Optic Transmission Standards

Another standard potentially important to LAN users is the fiber dis-tributed data interface, or FDDI. Developed primarily by ANSI, FDDI defines how electronic information is formatted and carried over fiber-optic cable. Widespread compliance with FDDI will allow manufacturers to develop varied LAN offerings that function in similar, predictable ways, thus facilitating the use of multivendor, fiber-optic LANs.

In many organizations, small LANs connected via twisted-pair cable are already being linked via backbones of fiber-optic cable. The com-bined acceptance by manufacturers of 10-base-T and FDDI could make building and linking Ethernet LANs easier, less expensive, and more popular than it now is. Delays are inherent in the development and ac-ceptance of any standards, but both 10-base-T and FDDI are sufficiently far along to constitute safe bets for interested LAN users and managers.

The synchronous optical network, or SONET, is another optical fiber standard. SONET governs high-speed data transmission over fiber-optic cable and is most relevant to those building very large networks, such as local and long-distance telephone companies. With SONET and FDDI becoming more widely adopted, you can expect to see more fiber-based network products appearing over the next year or two. Eventually, your LAN may have access to many local and wide area networks via optical fiber, FDDI, and SONET.

*M*ultivendor Network Standards

Standards are also emerging to facilitate the integration of multivendor networks. The best-known true standards for internetwork communications are the transmission control protocol and internet protocol, usually referred to collectively as *TCP/IP*. The United States government, the first and largest user of multivendor networks, has spurred development of TCP/IP for more than 20 years and requires compliance with the protocols from any vendor hoping to penetrate this lucrative market. As a result, a single version of TCP/IP is supported by all leading network vendors.

TCP/IP is also viewed as the most efficient path toward compliance with OSI, the open systems interconnect network scheme being developed and promoted by the ISO. Most computing and communications vendors comply, or are planning to comply, with the standards that comprise OSI, a development that should eventually lead to interoperability among a broad range of products and services, including LANs.

Thus, vendors are building upon the interoperability supplied by TCP/IP to reach the goals expressed in the OSI model of standard network communications. TCP/IP, along with other emerging standards, will aid greatly in the integration of LANs with larger networks such as MANs (metropolitan area networks) and WANs (wide area networks), as well as in the migration toward truly interoperable networks, the ultimate goal of OSI and the ISO.

*N*etwork Managment Standards

Vendors supporting TCP/IP have recognized the need for powerful, integrated network management tools. Many have endorsed SNMP, the simple network management protocol, as a standard method for passing network management information among diverse products. As TCP/IP networks migrate toward OSI or compliance, vendors are expected to move from SNMP to CMIS, the common management information services, and CMIP, the common management information protocol being added to the OSI suite of protocols. Most major vendors have already announced their intent to support CMIP and CMIS.

(Some vendors, including Novell and 3Com, have also announced support of a protocol called CMOT, or common management over

TCP/IP. CMOT has been promoted as an interim step between SNMP and full compliance with CMIP and CMIS. However, most vendors and users now seem prepared to move directly from SNMP to CMIP/CMIS. CMOT is therefore expected to play a minor role in LANs and other networks and likely does not require your attention.)

You may read or hear reports about conflicts among the various network management protocols and tools that appear and evolve over the next few months and years. Rest assured, however, that most leading vendors will offer extensive support of SNMP and CMIP/CMIS, eventually if not immediately. No network vendor with long-term vision can afford to ignore these protocols, because network management is becoming a top priority for more and more LAN builders. Because a well-managed network is a better and more efficient network, users have a stake in the evolution of network management standards as well.

Electronic Transmission Standards

Yet another standard—X.400—is likely to affect the ease of your network's use over the next few years. The X.400 standard is being developed and promoted primarily by the CCITT, a standards body with close ties to the ISO and the primary developers of the X.25 standard for packet-switching, mentioned in Chapter 1. (CCITT is a French abbreviation that reflects the body's European heritage. A rough English translation is Consultative Committee on International Telephony and Telegraphy.)

Compliance with X.400 allows easy interconnection of electronic mail systems from diverse vendors. This standard is being supported by purveyors of both public e-mail services, such as AT&T Mail and MCI Mail, and private e-mail networks, such as IBM's PROFS and Digital Equipment's ALL-IN-1. As more vendors support X.400, the number of people you can reach via e-mail will continue to grow, and you will be able to communicate long distance as easily as you can with a nearby colleague.

X.400 is already widely supported, but an important companion standard is not so far along. This standard, called X.500, will allow easy access to the user directories of diverse e-mail systems and networks. When X.500 is widely supported, you should be able to find the e-mail address of a user on another network as easily as you can find colleagues on the network you use.

AT&T, Banyan, and other vendors already promote their own interim solutions to the problem of remote directories. Most vendors are expected to evolve their solutions into X.500-compatible offerings or to simply wait for X.500 to address the problem. One way or another, though, the odds are good that your e-mail solution will comply with at least X.400 over the next year, and with X.500 within another year or two.

User Interface Standards

Emerging standards also will affect other areas important to your LAN. One of these is the user interface, or appearance of your screen. As mentioned earlier in this book, IBM-compatible PCs are taking on characteristics—in particular, graphical user interfaces, or GUIs—previously restricted to Macintosh computers and advanced workstations.

With a common GUI, users can use the same or similar commands to manipulate all applications. The GUI can therefore eliminate the need to learn and remember completely different sets of basic commands for each application.

As discussed previously, the UNIX community is still trying to agree on a standard GUI. DOS environments lack a standard GUI as well, mostly because older DOS-based machines simply don't have the power to run applications and support an extensive GUI without unacceptably slow system performance.

Thus, some IBM-compatible PCs run Microsoft Windows, and some use interfaces, such as Quarterdeck's DesqView, that depend less on graphics. Meanwhile, IBM and Microsoft promote the graphical Presentation Manager as the user interface of choice for systems based on OS/2.

Meanwhile, Tandy Corporation promotes a user interface called DeskMate that comes with several built-in applications such as a note pad and a calculator. Several manufacturers of DOS-based applications, including Lotus Development, now sell versions of their products that can be launched (or started) and manipulated from DeskMate.

Tandy's great success in the IBM-compatible PC market, especially in schools, means that DeskMate will be supported by more software developers over the coming months. Although DeskMate is likely to remain a popular solution in academic settings, offerings from IBM, Microsoft, and other key vendors are expected to be more widely used in corporate environments.

*P*rinter Standards

Printers are also affected by standards. Currently, the biggest debate concerns printers that are compatible with PostScript, the page description language developed by Adobe Systems and considered a standard in the Macintosh world. However, PostScript compatibility is truly important only to users who must print large volumes of graphics. For text and numbers, non-PostScript printers are usually more than adequate, as well as less expensive.

A Caveat

In viewing any standard, remember that standards are just another technology and should be treated as such. That is, users and managers should not select standards, but solutions. If those solutions also meet industry standards, so much the better. However, if the better solutions are nonstandard, they may be worthwhile anyway and can probably be made compatible with standards after your principal problem is solved.

Remember that the Macintosh computer was decidedly nonstandard when it was introduced, but that didn't stop users and managers from embracing it. No LAN user or managers should set out to avoid industry standards. Neither should anyone avoid potential solutions just because they don't adhere to standards that may prove to be irrelevant to the specifics of your situation.

*Y*our Role in Your Network's Future

A basic characteristic of networks is that they grow and change. As a LAN user, you are closely linked to changes in your network, both as an observer and as an active participant in these changes.

In 1972, Gregory Bateson, a psychiatrist and behavioral scientist who was a colleague of the people who created the theories that made electronic computers possible, published a collection of works, titled *Steps to an Ecology of Mind.* Bateson says that people's minds, and the minds of groups of people, form an ecology. Everything is connected, and everything that happens can affect the entire connected system. Sounds a lot like your LAN and your organization, doesn't it?

One of Bateson's other basic tenets also applies to LANs. Bateson says that people should realize that reality is not necessarily what they believe it is, a viewpoint that certainly applies to LANs. Especially when users and managers confront decisions about joining, building, or enhancing a LAN, beliefs must be carefully balanced with reality, especially in the face of skillful marketing.

Sometimes, for example, PC users in groups long to be connected to a nearby LAN. Once connected, though, they find that they can do little work they couldn't do before, and their PCs respond more slowly than before. Similar disappointments occur to users who request or implement enhancements without careful evaluations to balance their beliefs.

Someday you may believe you need a more powerful PC or some other enhancement. You and your colleagues may decide your LAN is too slow and needs upgrading. In cases like these, get as much hard information as you can to support your beliefs, so your managers can make their best case for you to their managers. You and your colleagues should evaluate carefully everything you believe (including all the suggestions in this book) when it involves changes to your LAN.

The quality of your LAN directly affects the quality of the skills and experience you acquire as a user of that LAN. Those skills and experiences, in turn, directly affect the progress of your career, which affects your satisfaction with your life. Therefore, your active participation in the health and growth of your LAN is as much in your best interests as it is your organization's managers.

Some of the ways in which you can participate are described in the earlier sections of this chapter. In addition, you and your colleagues must take advantage of opportunities to speak up about your LAN and your needs now and in the future. Talk to both your managers and vendor representatives whenever appropriate. You are the vital link between the managers who shape your network and the vendors who provide its parts. You're the one who uses everything all the time—that's why you're called a user. Your input is essential to managers and vendors if your network is to do its best work for you and your organization. Those who are best at their jobs will listen and take your comments to heart, especially when your comments are augmented by well-documented facts.

To speak up intelligently, you must also listen, particularly to events and trends that affect your network and organization. After all, if you want to be heard, you must speak intelligently. To prepare you, three invaluable resources are available to you: user groups, user-oriented education, and industry-related publications.

*J*oining User Groups

If more than 10 people use a particular computing or LAN product near you, then a user group for that product probably already meets regularly. For example, across the country and around the world, user groups exist for Novell NetWare, Apple Macintosh Computers, and UNIX systems. You may find local groups through the business section of your local paper or a locally produced computing publication. Otherwise, contact your local vendor or call the product manufacturer directly and find out how to contact the groups focused on the products that interest you.

User groups are usually inexpensive to join and can be very valuable. Membership often includes a periodic newsletter and frequent presentations of new or enhanced products by vendors. They also include discussion among users in many situations, including situations similar to yours. The people you meet at user groups can become valuable resources as well.

*A*ttending Classes and Seminars

In addition to user groups, you can probably find seminars or classes in LAN-related topics offered by consultants, vendors, colleges, or schools in your area. Some of these may be free, and others may offer continuing education units (CEUs) or actual college credit. Don't forget to find out if any of these qualify for any tuition assistance your organization may offer.

Classes, tutorials, panels, and presentations almost always accompany computing industry trade shows and conferences. These are often broader than locally offered courses, but can be ideal for brief overviews of specific products or topics. At events that span multiple days, more detailed tutorials may be offered, some of which offer CEUs (and charge tuition). User groups from different states or regions often have collective meetings at these events as well, providing an opportunity for you to expand your contacts with other users.

Make sure to use discretion in selecting the classes and seminars you attend. Even those that are free take time away from your primary work, so be selective. Call the organizer or instructor with any specific questions you have about what you will learn (or will be expected to know).

Perhaps most important, work with your managers to examine carefully the benefits of the classes that interest you and to lobby for assistance in attending classes or seminars that are expensive or in distant locations. Work equally closely with your colleagues to share what you learn and to put your new-found knowledge to its best use in your work group.

*R*eading, Reading, Reading

One more source of information is the wide range of industry-related books, magazines, and newsletters in existence today. Some magazines even offer on-line bulletin boards, so you can receive programs and articles via computer and modem. If your local newspaper offers regular features or sections on business or technology, these may be worth reading. Public Television and some cable TV networks offer computing-related programs as well.

The industry publications that can help you may not be those only from the computing industry. Your organization's business may have its own trade journals, which may be more than worth your while to read. Often such publications contain articles or interviews that discuss network issues you and your colleagues may face. Even if they don't, they can help you refine your views of the context within which you work.

You Make the Difference

As you and your network grow and change, so does the importance of your participation in your network's direction. Remember: If your network doesn't meet your needs, neither it nor you are going to be as productive as you and your organization want. Getting managers and vendors to attend to your needs, combined with your attending to the needs of your managers and organization, will result in the best possible LAN, in the hands of the best possible users.

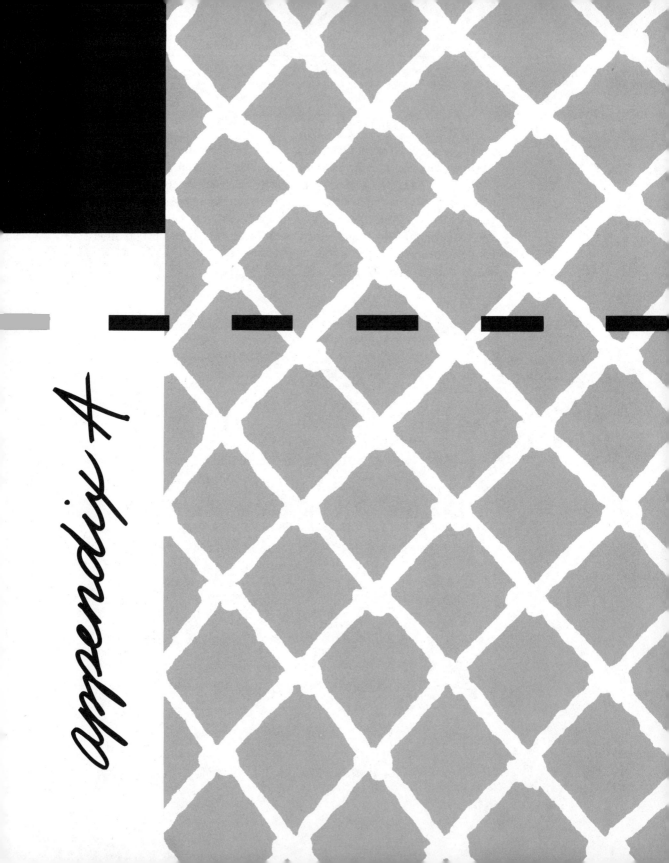

Appendix A

A

Tips for Using the DOS Programs BACKUP and RESTORE

BACKUP and RESTORE are two of the many supplementary programs that come with most versions of DOS from IBM and other vendors. As their names imply, BACKUP and RESTORE safeguard the data on your hard disk drive. You use BACKUP to make backup copies on floppy disks. Then you use these floppy disks with the RESTORE program to recreate what was on your hard disk before a system failure or similar disaster occurred.

If you're using DOS 3.2 or an earlier version, you probably have BACKUP and RESTORE on your hard disk or on the floppy disks that came with your DOS software. If you're using a newer version of DOS, you probably have the program XCOPY. In this case, use XCOPY to make and use your backup floppy disks, as discussed in Chapter 5 (you can then skip this section). This appendix offers users of earlier DOS versions a few tips about using BACKUP and RESTORE.

*P*reparing to Use BACKUP

Before you try to use BACKUP, first determine the version of DOS your PC uses. At the DOS prompt, type **ver** (for *version*) and press the ↵ key. Your screen should display a line of text similar to this: *IBM Personal Computer DOS Version 3.1*. The exact display depends on the version of DOS you are using and the manufacturer that supplied DOS for your system. If such a display does not appear on your screen, check your documentation or consult your PC or LAN manager to determine the version of DOS on your system.

If your system uses a version of DOS with a number that starts with 2 or 3, BACKUP is likely available to you. Your next step is to find the BACKUP program on your disk.

If your PC's hard disk has subdirectories and one is devoted to DOS, go to that subdirectory from the DOS prompt by typing **CD*subdirectory-name*** (replacing *subdirectory-name* with the name of the subdirectory you want to find) and pressing the ↵ key. Once you get to where the DOS programs are on your hard disk, search the subdirectory for a program called BACKUP.EXE or BACKUP.COM.

If you still cannot find BACKUP, just type **BACKUP** and press the ↵ key. If your screen responds with a message like *Bad command or file* *name,* then BACKUP is not in the subdirectory you're currently using. Try looking in other subdirectories, checking your documentation, or asking your system manager. If a message like *Invalid number of parameters* appears, BACKUP is actually in the directory you're using; you just need to correctly specify the command to find it.

Once you've found the BACKUP program, you must perform one more task before you can use it. You must format enough floppy disks to hold all the information on your hard disk. This task has two steps. First you must determine how much information is on your hard disk. To do this, from the DOS prompt that shows the letter of your hard disk drive, type **chkdsk** and press the ↵ key. After a few seconds, a display like this should appear:

```
21204992 bytes total disk space
38912 bytes in   2 hidden files
98304 bytes in  43 directories
12533760 bytes in 978 user files
8534016 bytes available on disk

655360 bytes total memory
194960 bytes free
```

Write down the number of bytes in hidden files, directories, and user files and add these three numbers to determine how many bytes of information are to be copied onto floppy disks. In this example, the amount is 38,912 + 98,304 + 12,533,760 = 12,670,976 bytes.

Next, divide this sum by the number of bytes each of your floppy disks can hold and round the result up to the next highest number. If you're using an XT-class computer, your 5.25-inch floppy disks each hold a maximum of 360,000 bytes. If you're using an AT-class computer, your floppy disks hold either 1,200,000 or 1,440,000 bytes each. Assuming an XT-class computer in our example, 12,670,976 ÷ 360,000 = 35.20. Thus, you need 36 floppy disks to make a complete backup copy of the hard disk in this example. If you're not sure how many bytes your floppy disks hold, check your system documentation, ask a colleague, or format a floppy disk and check the screen display when the formatting is complete. The screen display will indicate the number of bytes available.

Once you've arrived at the number of floppy disks you need, you must format them all before launching the BACKUP program. If you run out of formatted floppy disks while BACKUP is in process, you'll have to abort your backup operation, format the necessary disks, and start all over again. You might be able to format your disks on a colleague's system, but not all floppy disks work interchangeably. You therefore should format more floppy disks than you think you'll need, just to make sure.

Follow the instructions in your DOS or system documentation for formatting floppy disks. Make sure to format these disks without choosing the option for copying DOS onto them, or each floppy disk will hold less than its maximum capacity, increasing your risk of running out of formatted disks before the backup operation is complete.

Only after you've completed the preceding steps can you use the BACKUP program safely and successfully. Although most DOS documentation discusses these steps, the BACKUP program itself provides no on-screen assistance or warnings, so you must be prepared. Note that software offerings such as Gazelle Systems' Back-It, discussed in Chapter 5, provide helpful features not found in BACKUP, such as automatic computation of the number of floppy disks you'll need and the ability to format unformatted floppy disks during the backup process.

Using BACKUP (and RESTORE)

The BACKUP program offers several options, which are explained in your DOS documentation. If you use subdirectories, the most important of these is the /S option, which instructs BACKUP to copy files from all your subdirectories. If you want to make a backup copy of a specific directory on your hard disk, use BACKUP without the /S option and type the complete name of the directory, including the letter that designates the hard disk.

Most of BACKUP's other options allow you to make backup copies of files that have been changed after a certain date or time. If you make personal backup copies of your hard disk regularly, you will not need to use these options. In fact, using these options to make partial backup copies can cause confusion if you don't keep careful records of all changes you make on your hard disk and when those changes occur.

Be sure to label each backup floppy disk carefully and completely with the date the backup copy was made and a number that indicates the order in which each floppy disk was used: for example, "Disk 1 of 36," "Disk 2 of 36," and so on. This information is essential if you are to avoid confusion among multiple sets of backup disks. It also is essential whenever you use RESTORE.

Ideally, you should never have to use RESTORE. However, should you need to reconstruct the information on your hard disk, use the RESTORE /S option to restore every subdirectory on your backup disks. Also, be sure to specify the letter of the floppy disk drive from which RESTORE is to read information from your backup floppy disks. Again, note that Back-It and similar offerings provide easy-to-use menus and commands that make restoring from backup disks much easier than with RESTORE. (Chapter 5 presents detailed guidelines for making and maintaining personal backup copies.)

Appendix B

B

Industry Guidelines for Virus Prevention and Systems Reliability

In September 1988, representatives from several vendors gathered to develop guidelines to help network managers and users prevent viruses and make their networks more reliable. These guidelines have been adopted by more than 60 manufacturers, including Banyan, 3Com, Microsoft, and Novell. This appendix presents these guidelines, as published by the Strategic Workshop on Distributed Systems Reliability, hosted by the National LAN Laboratory on September 8, 1988, in Vail, Colorado.

Viruses and System Reliability

Computer viruses have become an important issue for computer vendors and users. While viruses are a risk to only a small percentage of computer systems, that risk must be addressed as part of industry concern for overall system reliability.

A computer virus is a program that is introduced into a computer system surreptitiously, often with malicious intent, masquerading as a normal system or application program. Viruses are often members of a larger family called "Trojan horse" programs. Viruses have the special (and dangerous) ability to reproduce themselves and propagate themselves to other systems, proliferating undetected. Both viruses and Trojan horse programs can damage your system in ways that range from merely consuming storage space to compromising data security and destroying data and programs.

The possibility of virus contamination can never be totally eliminated. The following procedures are aimed at reducing the risk. Depending on the sensitivity and/or value of the systems' software and data, procedures can be instituted to virtually eliminate the virus risk. As with any security measures, however, eliminating the risk means reducing users' access to the system and increasing administrative costs. The level of protection should be weighed against the need and the cost of the solution.

The best protection against virus contamination is a systems approach to reliability. These are some specific recommendations.

User Recommendations

- All software should be purchased from known, reputable sources.

- All purchased software should be in its original shrink wrap or sealed diskette containers when received.

- Backup copies of all original software should be made as soon as the software package is opened. Backup copies should be stored off site.

- Once purchased, all software should be reviewed carefully by a system manager, before it is installed on a distributed system (like a LAN).

- New software should be quarantined on an isolated computer. This testing will greatly reduce the risk of system virus contamination.

- A backup copy of all system software and data should be made at least once a month, with the backup copy stored for at least one year before reuse. This will allow restoration of a system that has been contaminated by a "time-released" virus. A plan that includes "grandfathered" rotation of backup copies will reduce risk even further.

- System administrators should restrict access to system programs and data on a "need-to-use" basis. This isolates problems, protects critical applications, and facilitates problem diagnosis.

- All programs on a system should be checked regularly for size changes. Any size deviations could be evidence of tampering or virus infiltration.

- Many "shareware" and "freeware" programs are invaluable applications. However, these programs are the prime entry point for system viruses. Skeptical review of such programs is prudent. Also, extended preliminary quarantine is essential before these programs are introduced on a distributed system.

- Any software that exhibits symptoms of possible virus contamination should be removed from general use immediately. System managers should develop plans for quick removal from service of all copies of a suspect program and immediate backup of all related data. These plans should be made known to all users and tested and reviewed periodically.

A Systems Approach to Reliability

Today's computer users require greater system reliability. If your business runs on computers, if your employees require computers to do their jobs, if you need computers to serve your customers properly, then reliable systems are critical to your business. Reliability is achieved by implementing several complementary strategies. The following is a set of proposed industry guidelines for users.

Analysis and Planning

Every successful distributed system installation requires both site and risk analysis, and creation of a plan for disaster recovery. Analyses and plans must be reviewed periodically.

System Administration

Every reliable distributed system should have an assigned administrator. The training needed by that administrator depends on the unique requirements of the distributed system and on the available resources.

There is a growing need for personnel trained in distributed systems and reliability. Vendors and users must support development of effective training programs to increase the number of trained personnel available in the future.

Power Quality Assurance

Many reliability problems stem from poor electrical power quality. Most of these problems can be prevented easily and economically. Distributed computer systems require clean, computer-grade power, free from the transients, spikes, brownouts, and blackouts typical of commercial-grade power.

Servers, communications components, and critical workstations should have battery backup power and may benefit from intelligent power protections. All network components need conditioned power. The level of protection to be implemented depends upon each organization's software and hardware reliability requirements.

Data Disaster Recovery Planning

Data backup and off-site storage should be an assigned task with continuing management supervision. Backup copies of all applications programs should be stored off site, in both their original and user-configured versions. At a minimum, there should be an incremental daily backup of system data, with complete backups of system disks performed at a frequency determined by the criticality of the data and applications.

The convenience of automated backup can pay off in added reliability. Established procedures for test and verification of backup data are also necessary.

Redundancy

All hardware and software components are subject to periodic failure. These failures can be the result of component deterioration, environmental conditions, or misuse. Some components are not critical to system operations, and some can be easily replaced. But if a component's failure will cause unacceptable downtime, then an identical, redundant component should be integrated into the system. That redundant component provides a system feature known as fault tolerance, taking over and continuing normal operations in the event of a primary component failure.

Risk analysis will help determine the need for fault tolerance. Risk analysis also permits identification of particular system components where fault tolerance is a cost-effective reliability strategy.

For systems where downtime is not a critical issue, a policy for purchase and inventory of redundant components can provide cost-effective system reliability. Redundancy can be as simple as having tested spare runs of cable installed to be used in case of a wiring defect or having a spare workstation, disk drive, or memory card available for installation in case of a component failure.

Management Tools

Reliable hardware components alone do not guarantee a reliable system. Equally necessary are software utilities to manage the hardware. Easy-to-use software tools for system management make local management easier for professionals and users and are absolutely necessary for remote management. These utilities monitor system health, provide warnings of potential problems, and help managers locate problems quickly.

Systems that grow to require large subnetworks, or systems that are geographically dispersed, cannot be economically staffed with specialists at every site. Many important network management functions can be accomplished remotely with hardware and software tools. A systems approach using tools such as these can greatly enhance reliability.

Distributed System Management

The ease of installation and usability of distributed systems have been responsible for the rise of the myth that these dispersed systems, especially systems of PCs, do not need management. In fact, every system whose resources are shared by multiple users requires management. Computing is changing from several professionals managing a single computer to single professionals managing multiple computers in distributed environments. In these new environments, innovative management is essential.

A focus on system reliability is mandatory in today's computing environments. Reliable systems pay off in more effective use of resources, more efficient business operations, and more satisfied customers. System reliability in distributed environments requires a combination of hardware, software, and management commitment.

Appendix C

Cabling Issues

(Much of the material in this appendix was originally written for "The Datacom Agenda," a course in data communications basics developed in collaboration with McDowell-Romero Communications Consultants of Carmel Valley, California. The material is used with McDowell-Romero's gracious permission.)

As mentioned in Chapter 2, network media present managers and users with a potentially bewildering array of options and pitfalls. These are compounded by the high costs of cabling and installation in some areas and by the unpredictability of most networks. Cabling is the source of many common LAN problems, and short-term or off-the-shelf cabling schemes are often inadequate as long-term solutions.

LAN users and managers need easy-to-use, flexible connections; graceful growth and expansion capabilities, and maximum economy from their networks. Meeting these requirements calls for a cabling strategy as well implemented and well considered as the rest of a work group's network schemes. When well-designed and well-implemented, LAN cabling strategies provide support for flexible, economical information networks. Such strategies can also support future distributed architectures, such as those required for true client-server computing.

Thus, network users need strategies and plans specific to their premises and enterprises to tie their various network media together into flexible, future-proof, unified cabling schemes suited to meet today's and tomorrow's data communications needs. The more complete and coherent users and managers can make the cabling plans for all their premises, the more current and future costs and problems can be eliminated or reduced.

As with other aspects of network building, assessment and planning are the cornerstones of any cabling plan. Cabling assessment and planning can help avoid problems for users, managers, vendors, and support providers. For example, a well-considered cabling plan will help avoid installation of cable too close to electrical wiring, lighting fixtures, or other potential sources of interference that can garble or interrupt network transmissions. Such details must be addressed in each work group's cabling plan.

Before specific details can be addressed, each work group cabling plan must address some basic issues. Some of these issues are defined by the network technologies chosen or the characteristics of the facilities being wired. Resolution of basic issues requires cooperation among users, managers, vendors, and consultants. The following paragraphs discuss some considerations common to any work group cabling plan.

*W*hat Cabling to Use?

As discussed in Chapter 2, there are many different types of LAN cabling, each with its own strengths, weaknesses, and economies. Although different LAN offerings can operate with a variety of media, there is an apparent link between LAN performance and LAN media.

Typically, lower-cost, limited-performance basic LANs depend primarily on twisted-pair cabling. LANs that are moderate in price and performance tend to use shielded baseband (low bandwidth) coaxial cable, and high-cost, high-performance LANs tend to use broadband (high bandwidth) coaxial cable, baseband coaxial cable, or shielded twisted-pair cabling.

In general, shielded twisted-pair cabling is most effective when used to connect no more than 100 computers, operating over distances of no more than several thousand feet at speeds of no more than 16 megabits per second. Most coaxial cable can carry signals effectively for distances of up to several miles, which makes coaxial cable a good choice for larger networks. Most professional cable installers are far more experienced with coaxial and twisted-pair cable than other types of cable, another important consideration for your work group's cabling strategy.

*W*hose Cabling to Use?

Almost every LAN offering comes with specific recommendations regarding the types of cable to use. Some products come with actual cables. At the same time, most work groups exist in buildings where some type of wiring already is in place, usually supporting a telephone system or some other form of electronic communication. Integrated cabling solutions designed for use throughout entire facilities also are available. Examples include AT&T's Systimax PDS, IBM's Cabling

System, and Digital Equipment Corporation's DECnet, all of which are described later in this appendix.

The cables that come with a particular LAN offering are usually best for that offering, but they may not be easy to integrate into a work group's or organization's overall cabling scheme. In many cases, other, less expensive cabling alternatives also can be used effectively. For example, many third-party offerings allow replacement of coaxial cable with shielded or unshielded twisted-pair cable. The convenience of vendor-supplied cabling must be weighed carefully against that cabling's costs and compatibility with other solutions in use by other work groups or elsewhere within an enterprise.

As discussed in Chapter 2, the use of in-place cabling carries special risks, including insufficient capacity and reliability to support critical LAN applications. Vendor-supplied large-scale solutions can be expensive and may not be equally compatible with the LAN solutions chosen by every work group. Also, integrated solutions tend to reflect the strengths and weaknesses of their vendors and to be less well suited to work groups in smaller organizations.

In many cases, the cables supplied with or recommended by a group's chosen LAN vendor are the most convenient solution. These individual solutions can be linked later via coaxial or fiber-optic cable backbones and associated connection devices. Such an approach is often more economical to implement and easier to upgrade than an integrated approach as needs within individual work groups evolve. This apparently fragmented approach is also often easier to use when linking existing networks than is a more unified approach that requires extensive replacement of cabling already in use.

*W*here to Put Cabling?

In creating a unified cabling plan, another important issue is where all the network wiring will actually run within a work group's or enterprise's building. There are three basic cable-routing alternatives inside any building. Cable can be run under floors, over ceilings, or along floors and walls through what are called *surface raceways*. Most cabling plans include combinations of all three of these choices.

Cabling installed under floors is usually housed in steel ducts or trenches. These make cables difficult to tap and resistant to breaks, cuts, or other damage. When trenches are included in the design of a building, they provide maximum physical and electrical protection.

Cable conduits built under floors can be initially more expensive than other alternatives and can present difficulties if significant network expansion or changes are required. Raised floors with open-air cable runs placed beneath them can provide more flexibility, but may not comply with local fire codes.

The complement to under-floor cabling is over-ceiling cabling, where cables typically travel along routes parallel to those used by power cables or partitions that divide modular offices. The flexibility and relative economy of over-ceiling cabling make this alternative very popular. However, conduits for air conditioning, lighting, and power already occupy much of the space above the ceilings in many buildings. The remaining space may be inadequate for LAN cables in some locations within your enterprise.

With surface raceways, cables are usually run along the outer edges of room floors and covered by metal conduits that are attached at the room's baseboards. Although surface raceways can be easily installed almost anywhere, and provide superior protection from electromagnetic interference, they are difficult to move or modify in the face of network growth or changes.

Surface raceways also require links to users' desktops. These are usually provided with flat, ribbon cable or within raised, flexible conduits attached to the floor of a room. Shoes with sharp high heels have been known to slice through ribbon cable, and office workers can trip over floor-mounted wiring conduits, so these alternatives must be considered and implemented carefully.

Other cabling options will likely appear. However, for those who need to make cabling decisions today, the safest choice is *plenum* cable. Plenum cable is designed to be installed in a building's existing air ducts and is therefore specially insulated to burn slowly, produce no toxic gases, and resist kinks when bent. Less expensive cables, especially those insulated with polyvinyl chloride (PVC), become highly poisonous when they burn or melt, compounding your risk during a fire.

Plenum cable is usually more expensive than other cable types. Nonetheless, it is expected to remain the best all-around cable buy for some time to come, even for networks where cable is not installed in air ducts.

No matter what type of cable your group chooses or where it's installed, users and managers must cooperate to develop and maintain an accurate, complete map of your cable installations. These records are invaluable tools in identifying and solving problems and in expanding a network efficiently and economically.

*W**ho's Responsible for Cabling?*

Another set of important cabling issues relate to cabling responsibility. Often, a network manager must work with several LAN or cabling vendors, a cable installation firm, individual users, department managers, and others to implement a cabling plan. These relationships are complex and must be well-managed if they are to work.

In particular, responsibility for installating, moving, changing, inventorying, and regularly testing cables and resolving cabling problems must be assigned to specific parties and rigorously enforced. Assigning responsiblity is particularly important to work groups or enterprises in leased facilities because responsibility for cable maintenance and repair may vary with the cable's location. This issue is made more complex if your group leases lines for LAN transmission or network-to-network connections.

In most areas, cabling that links the floors of a building is the responsibility of the building owner or manager, and cabling that links facilities on a floor is the responsibility of individual tenant organizations or work groups. However, managers must work with their LAN and cabling consultants to document specific responsibilities. Managers must then communicate clearly with users, so they understand their responsibilities and contact the right people when problems arise.

Some Cabling Details

In planning a cabling strategy, you must attend to many details that may seem trivial, but that in fact are critical to the reliable operation of your system. For example, every flexible network cabling scheme depends on wire closets, where cable terminations and connections can be managed and protected centrally. Wire closets must be located intelligently and labeled clearly. They must also be well-documented in your organization's cable map. Sufficient wall plates and jacks must also be installed in your work group's facilities to accommodate growth and changes in your LAN.

Another important cable installation issue is grounding of the cabling system. A ground is an electrical path designed to disperse high-voltage electrical spikes, usually by routing them into the earth near a facility. Grounding issues are typically addressed in a network's design, if not by the manufacturers of the particular hardware and software being supported.

Documentation for specific products should be examined carefully to determine whether a product has special grounding requirements. Otherwise, the best practice is to ignore grounding unless a problem appears. Every cabling system should be grounded at only one point. Multiple grounding points can create electrical interference that defeats your cabling's shielding.

Cable weight and placement is another consideration. For example, make sure cable installers don't allow cables to support the weight of connected devices, such as signal amplifiers or splitters. Each device must rest on or be attached to a part of the building or duct around the cable if its connection to the cable is to be reliable.

The weight of each cable segment is itself a consideration. Weight support should be provided every 15 to 20 feet of cable to prevent cable sags from decreasing a cable's reliability and life.

All cable ends must be tightly sealed, and all unused cable ends must be properly terminated. These steps help reduce the likelihood of accidental groundings, shorts, or other transient electrical problems that can be maddeningly difficult to identify and isolate. Lengths of cable are available with connectors already attached to their ends. These can save significant time and money at installation and can also increase reliability by reducing the number of questionable connections installed in your network.

Every cable has a manufacturers' stated maximum bend radius and pulling force. These limits must be determined for every cable segment and should never be exceeded. As a general rule, bends in cable should not be greater than five times the diameter of that cable. This rule holds true for your cable installers as well as for you and your colleagues when you move your connected devices around your offices.

Cable must also be installed so that it is twisted and sharply bent as little as possible. With coaxial cable, the distance between the shield and the center conductor determines the cable's impedance, a type of electrical interference. Kinking can bring the center conductor close enough to the shield to partially or completely impede transmission.

Even though twisted-pair cable is almost impervious to damage from kinking, it also should be installed with a minimum of twists. Installing cable in segments helps reduce twists and kinks considerably. These steps help avoid hidden breaks and other physical cable faults.

All cable must be pretested, or tested for integrity before it is installed. Pretesting helps you avoid the troublesome situation in which a cable section is installed, tested, and then found faulty and must be removed before it has even been put into service. For the same reasons, every cable should be visually inspected before installation.

Just as cable should be installed in manageable segments, so should it be tested. Cable testing should focus on two important areas: continuity, or lack of faults that impede transmission; and transmission loss, including leaks, breaks, and faulty insulation. With broadband cable systems, transmission and return losses should be analyzed with a device called a sweep generator.

After cable is actually installed, enterprises need to develop and enforce standard procedures for regularly testing and inventorying cable, isolating problems, and connecting different devices. These procedures themselves must be audited and updated periodically, with the cooperation of all relevant suppliers, managers and users.

*H*ow Major Vendors Are Addressing Cabling Issues

Leading network vendors have themselves developed various responses to customers' needs for unified wiring and distribution. A look at the main characteristics of the systems from IBM, AT&T, and Digital Equipment Corporation—the systems you are most likely to encounter—will show you the broad range of possible responses to common issues, and how existing resources can be used (by users and vendors) to create effective, unified distributions systems.

*T*he IBM Cabling System

As expected given IBM's stature in the computing industry, the IBM Cabling System is rapidly evolving into a de facto standard network cabling solution. Though considered expensive and complex by some, the IBM Cabling System is comprehensive and well integrated. It is also evolving, to provide more economical and flexible cabling alternatives.

The IBM Cabling System is designed for star networks. Examples include the IBM Token-Ring (which uses star topology) and PC Networks, most host-terminal data communications setups, and telephone systems (such as those sold by IBM's former ROLM subsidiary, now jointly owned by IBM and Siemens). At the center of each star is a wiring closet, with the wiring closets themselves wired together at a central distribution point.

The most interesting components of the IBM Cabling System may be the IBM-designed data connectors. Standard RS-232, RS-449, coaxial, and RJ-11 telephone-type connectors all have gender—some are "male," some are "female"—and links between connectors of the same gender require connectors called gender changers. IBM's connectors are genderless; any connector can be plugged into any other. This permits simpler connections between devices and at wall plates, which can be configured with IBM connectors or RJ-11 jacks for telephone-system support.

IBM's Cabling System also uses several different types of cable, each of which is UL (Underwriters Laboratories) and ETL (Electronic Testing Laboratory) approved. For data communications only, the system uses IBM Type I cable, which carries two pairs of shielded, twisted-pair copper wires. For both data and voice transmission, the system uses Type II cable. Type II cable contains six pairs of wires. Two pairs are shielded and are designed for data. The other four unshielded pairs are for voice transmissions.

To support the 4-megabit-per-second version of the Token-Ring LAN, the system uses Type III cable, which is smaller and far less expensive than Type I or II cable. Type III cable contains two or four unshielded twisted pair of copper wire.

However, IBM does not recommend the use of unshielded twisted-pair cable for high-speed data communications. Because of this, and the fact that Type III cable was not designed by IBM, the cable is not supported by IBM as enthusiastically as the other types.

For under-carpet use and the making of patch cords, the system uses Type V cable. Type V cable contains two multimode optical fibers, each of which is of the industry-standard 100/140-micron type.

Still other cable types are expected to appear as network and transmission technologies evolve; IBM has left gaps in its numbering system to accommodate at least some of these. In addition, numerous manufacturers, including Belden and Control Cable, are licensed to sell and manufacture cable, connectors, and other equipment for the IBM Cabling System.

If an enterprise is committed to IBM network technology, especially the Token-Ring LAN or ROLM voice/data communications systems, the IBM Cabling System is an ideal solution. In some cases, IBM-type cabling can replace or be run alongside existing telephone wiring to prepare customer premises for future communications needs. However, customers committed to Ethernet LANs or other bus topologies are less likely to benefit from the IBM Cabling System.

The AT&T SYSTIMAX Premises Distribution System (PDS)

Reflecting its heritage as a telephone company, AT&T has devised a premises wiring system that makes extensive use of unshielded, twisted-pair copper wire—the medium of choice for telephone systems for most of the past 100 years. AT&T proposes to integrate voice and data applications through its Information Systems Architecture (ISA) and its support of the Integrated Services Digital Network (ISDN) and to integrate voice and data communications management via its Unified Network Management Architecture (UNMA). Similarly, the SYSTIMAX PDS is designed as an integrated solution for premises distribution of electronic information.

Under the SYSTIMAX PDS, star-shaped configurations of twisted-pair wiring have central wiring concentrators connected via a fiber-optic backbone, which AT&T calls the Premises Lightguide (or Lightwave) System. (Twisted-pair cable can be used for the backbone system if traffic demands do not warrant the investment in fiber.) With its fiber and copper combination, PDS supports connections to AT&T's Information Systems Network (ISN) and Starlan offerings, as well as to its advanced PBXs.

AT&T's experience with twisted-pair cable is reflected in the ability of PDS to support data transmissions from IBM 3270-compatible terminals, Wang workstations, and RS-232 interfaces. AT&T engineering allows SYSTIMAX PDS to carry data over unshielded twisted-pair cable as much as three times further than the maximum distances possible with IBM's Type 3 cable, according to some analysts.

AT&T has also devised several types of connectors and adapters for SYSTIMAX PDS. Connectors range in size from 8 to 50 pins, and adapters allow connections between different types and sizes of cable. Some adapters also match the different impedances of coaxial and twisted-pair cables, allowing easier connections between these two cable types. Twisted-pair connections among Wang and IBM devices via SYSTIMAX PDS are made possible by adapters designed by AT&T for these specific applications.

Unlike IBM's connectors, AT&T's connectors are based on existing connector technology. The PDS connector plugs into a standard, telephone-type modular jack equipped with eight-pin connections instead of the four-pin connections found on most single-line telephones. The eight pins are configured exactly the same way as AT&T's RJ48 jacks—the connections designated by the company for use in ISDN environments, as they emerge. AT&T claims that the use of this connector and its standard pin assignments allows network equipment to be easily moved from site to site.

AT&T has also designed what it calls a Universal Information Outlet, or UIO—basically, a jack within a jack. The outer jack, or base unit, is connected directly to the network transmission cable. The inner, plug-in jack accepts the plugs of connected devices. To plug a device with a new pin configuration into a UIO, a user needs to change only the inner jack and does not have to rewire the entire UIO, as would be necessary with a standard jack. The UIO is designed to support six- or eight-pin plug configurations and transmission speeds of up to 6 megabits per second.

AT&T's SYSTIMAX PDS is divided into six subsystems, which the firm claims are adequate to meet the wiring needs of all types of buildings and premises. This modular approach allows customers to upgrade their systems and to make changes when and where necessary without disrupting the entire network. The Work Location Subsystem provides the twisted-pair connection between desktops and wall plates. The Horizontal Subsystem connects Work Location Subsystem cables to the central wiring closet on a premises' floor.

The Riser Subsystem provides the floor-to-floor connections between Horizontal Subsystems using twisted-pair or fiberoptic cable. A Campus Subsystem offers the same choice of media for connections among multiple nearby buildings. The SYSTIMAX PDS Administration Subsystem acts as the central wiring closet for each building, housing facilities for central control and management of SYSTIMAX PDS. Finally, the Equipment Cabling Subsystem is used to connect mainframes or other central communications equipment to SYSTIMAX PDS via either twisted-pair or fiber-optic cable.

AT&T's SYSTIMAX PDS may be applicable to a wider range of facilities than IBM's Cabling System, especially given its support of connections to systems from other manufacturers. However, like the IBM Cabling System, AT&T's SYSTIMAX PDS is much more compatible with star-shaped communications networks than with bus-configured networks like Ethernet.

The Digital Equipment Corporation DECconnect System

Digital Equipment Corporation's DECconnect architecture for premises wiring is very different from IBM's and AT&T's in several interesting ways. For one, it is the product not of ambitious developers at Digital, but of demand from Digital's customers. This reflects Digital's long history of customers more technologically oriented than those of many other suppliers. Also, whereas the other schemes described in this appendix are less than optimal for Ethernet-like networks, DECconnect relies on Ethernet, running on coaxial or fiberoptic cable, to provide all connections.

Another difference is DECconnect's topology. Each floor in a building is wired with a star topology, with every floor's satellite equipment room connected via an Ethernet bus. Digital calls this scheme a radial topology and claims it provides maximum flexibility for premises cabling system designers.

Digital also takes a different approach to cabling itself. IBM and AT&T tend to promote use of single cables containing multiple wire pairs. Digital, in contrast, keeps transmission facilities physically separate. Each wall plate contains one wire pair for voice transmissions, one wire pair for asynchronous data communications at speeds up to 19.2 kilobytes per second, and one thin Ethernet cable for communication at speeds up to 10 megabytes per second. With the Ethernet transceivers all hidden behind the wall plates, users can plug into an Ethernet jack almost as easily as most people can plug in a single-line telephone.

However, Digital did use one nonstandard connector, for the asynchronous connection supported by DECconnect. Although this approach keeps users from confusing their telephone and asynchronous data plugs and jacks, some users and network builders complain about the use of any nonstandard connectors at all.

All of the shortcomings for Ethernet users that accompany solutions from IBM and AT&T disappear with DECconnect. In fact, DECconnect supports easier Ethernet connections than almost any other premises wiring architecture. However, DECconnect is not as efficient for users with significant commitments to star-topology LANs.

Choices and Costs

A complex unified cabling scheme can call for tens of thousands of feet of cabling, thousands of connectors and related devices, and weeks of planning and installation time. This all translates into significant potential costs, which must be analyzed and compared carefully before customers make their final purchase decisions.

In some environments, the total cost per connection will drive the decisions behind a cabling strategy. In others, it will be the cost per foot of distance to be covered. In still others it will be the specific costs of the cabling and its installation.

Network planners must not fall victim to easy but misleading cost comparisons. A prime example of such a comparison is per-station connection costs. In a hypothetical 128-station network, for instance, estimated costs for cabling and installation might be about $47,000, or $367 per station.

Using the same cabling and installation sources, a similar network of 1,500 stations would have a lower per-station connect cost—about $350—but would require a total investment of over half a million dollars. Clearly, the lowest per-station connection cost alone is an insufficient foundation for decisions about network cabling. Other costs must be included to build a total picture.

Broadband coaxial cable is less expensive per foot than baseband cable. Broadband prices range from $0.35 to $1.00 per foot, whereas baseband cable ranges from $0.50 to $3.00 per foot. In addition, baseband coaxial cable often must be run in hard, fireproof conduits such as metal pipes, to comply with fire laws, a requirement that can make the cost differences even greater. Broadband cable also requires expertise in radio-frequency (RF) technologies for design, installation, and maintenance, which baseband cable does not.

No work group or organization has sufficient resources to remain totally current on all possible cabling alternatives, their costs, and the market conditions that shape them. Vendors of cable, connectors, and related products, on the other hand, must keep track of the cabling marketplace to remain competitive. This makes cable and connector vendors ideal partners for users attempting to determine how best to meet their short- and long-term cabling plans.

Many organizations have already recognized the complexity of their network requirements and have developed network management staffs to cope with this complexity. As network needs grow and cabling options increase, more organizations will be able to justify the appointment of a full-time cabling manager to make sure cabling decisions are made in step with network decisions. In the interim, cabling vendors, installers, and consultants can play valuable roles in helping you and your colleagues build and maintain the most reliable, dependable networks possible, today and tomorrow.

Other Considerations

The importance of a well-considered cabling plan can't be over-emphasized, especially for work groups that are parts of larger organizations and groups that work frequently with other LAN-using groups. Whether for a room, a single building, or a multibuilding campus, a network cabling plan must reflect careful consideration of users' needs and an organization's resources, especially those unique to a particular environment or group of users.

In addition to the issues discussed in the preceding paragraphs, a unified cabling plan must take into account such diverse influences as user and contractor safety, applicable regulations, network performance needs, facilities security, and the availability of rights of way in areas where distribution facilities are desired. Further, those developing cabling plans for LANs must work with those within the same organization responsible for the cabling related to telephones, mainframe computers, minicomputers, and other communications resources. These steps are necessary if a cabling plan is to be truly integrated.

A complex, unified cabling scheme can call for tens of thousands of feet of cabling, thousands of connectors and related devices, and weeks of planning and installation time—at significant potential costs. Thus, cabling schemes must be analyzed and compared carefully before a final purchase decision is made.

In addition, in finally arriving at an estimate of the amount of cable needed, planners should most likely double or even triple their figures before cable installation actually begins. All networks grow, and no one can predict such growth exactly, so it's important to remember that new cabling can cost 10 times as much to install after all the carpets are laid and the company president's heavy mahogany desk is in place. In many cases, the most economical and future-proof solution is to install a network outlet everywhere a telephone or electrical outlet is located.

appendix D

D

LAN Resources

Numerous resources are available to help you learn more about LANs. This appendix discusses a few of these resources and provides brief comments about some of them. Your LAN reseller or consultant can provide you with additional suggestions for sources of help.

Magazines

Almost every computing-related publication carries some information about LANs. The magazines listed here will give almost any LAN user or manager a constant, varied supply of useful, accessible information without making reading a full-time job.

> *Computer Currents*
> 5720 Hollis Street
> Emeryville, CA 94608
> phone: 415/547-6800
> fax: 415/547-4613

A regional magazine, published twice a month in the San Francisco Bay Area and monthly in Southern California, Boston, Texas, and elsewhere, *Computer Currents* focuses on desktop computing. It includes a separate section on LANs. A list of user groups and bulletin board systems appears in each issue. This magazine is also valuable for comparing the offerings and prices of regional vendors, who account for most of the magazine's advertising. You can subscribe by mail, but the magazine is usually available for free from numerous computer retailers and other distribution points.

> *Connect* (The Journal of Computer Networking)
> 3Com Corporation
> 3165 Kifer Road
> Santa Clara, CA 95052-8145

Aimed primarily at information systems and data processing managers, but of great value to users as well, this magazine discusses issues of interest to all LAN users, even though it is published by 3Com. *Connect* is published quarterly and is available for free to those involved with computing networks. Contact your local 3Com representative or write, on your organization's letterhead, to the address listed here.

Data Communications
McGraw-Hill Information Services
McGraw-Hill Building
1221 Avenue of the Americas
New York, NY 10020
phone: 212/512-2000
fax: 212/512-6833

This magazine is considered a journal of record in the data communications and computing industries, like *The New York Times* or the *Washington Post* in journalistic and political circles. Some articles may be a bit beyond some users, but every issue contains at least a few useful and interesting articles for LAN users and managers. *Data Communications* often includes clear explanations of important technical and market issues.

Data Communications is published monthly, with additional issues appearing throughout the year, including an annual buyer's guide. Subscriptions are approximately $40 a year—and worth it.

InformationWeek (The Newsmagazine for
  Information Management)
CMP Publications, Inc.
600 Community Drive
Manhassett, NY 11030
phone: 516/562-5000
fax: 516/562-5474

InformationWeek is perhaps the closest thing to a slick, weekly business news magazine in computing. This publication focuses on the entire information industry, and its primary audience is information systems managers. However, its information is presented in a style and format that allows quick scanning and assimilation. It includes a section on network computing, frequent articles on vendor and user strategies, and industry news and analysis. *InformationWeek* is available at no cost to managers and professionals involved in information systems.

>   *LAN Times*
>   151 East 1700 South
>   Suite 100
>   Provo, UT 84606
>   phone: 801/379-5850
>   fax: 801/379-5509

This tabloid-format magazine is aimed primarily at LAN users and managers. When originally published by Novell, the primary emphasis was on that firm's products. Since McGraw-Hill purchased the magazine in 1989, its editorial focus has expanded to encompass news and events across the LAN industry. *LAN Times* is published monthly and is available at no charge to those involved with LANs.

>   *Network World* (The Newsweekly of User Networking Strategies)
>   Box 9171
>   375 Cochituate Road
>   Framingham, MA 01701-9171
>   phone: 508/820-2543
>   fax: 508/879-3167

A widely read, widely respected tabloid-format newspaper, *Network World* carries news and regular sections on data communications, local networking, and management strategies. A quick scan every week will complement your LAN-specific knowledge and keep you up-to-date. Available free to those involved with LANs or other communications systems.

>   *PC Magazine* (The Independent Guide to IBM-Standard Personal
>   Computing)
>   Ziff-Davis Publishing Company
>   One Park Avenue
>   New York, NY 10016
>   phone: 212/503-5255

This computing industry journal of record is a thick magazine published every two weeks. It includes numerous sections and articles of interest to LAN users and managers. It also offers frequent product analyses and comparisons. *PC Magazine* is available by subscription for about $40 a year or from many newsstands.

*N*ewsletters, Research Reports, and Seminars

Market research houses and newsletter publishers rarely issue products you can find on newsstands or purchase at low cost. However, these resources produce much more detailed and analytical information than is available from any typical trade publication. Professional newsletters also include no advertising.

Departments can often share subscriptions to these firms' offerings effectively and economically. Department managers should work with senior management to coordinate the most cost-effective way to take advantage of these resources.

The firms listed here offer too broad a range of reports, newsletters, and services to enumerate here. Contact each firm for a detailed listing of their current products and services so you can compare them before deciding which to try. Also, try to negotiate partial or total refunds if you and your colleagues are unsatisfied with the research or newsletters you purchase.

DataTrends Publications, Inc.
8130 Boone Boulevard
Suite 210
Vienna, VA 22182
phone: 703/760-0660
fax: 703/760-9365

DataTrends Publications publishes numerous newsletters, including *Netline, Network Management Systems & Strategies*, and *SNA Communications Report*. Prices average approximately $400 a year.

Forrester Research
185 Alewife Brook Parkway
Cambridge, MA 02138
phone: 617/497-7090
fax: 617/868-0577

Gartner Group, Inc.
56 Top Gallant Road
P.O. Box 10212
Stamford, CT 06904-2212
phone: 203/964-0096
fax: 203/324-7901

International Data Corporation
Five Speen Street
Framingham, MA 01701
phone: 508/872-8200

McDowell-Romero Communications Consultants
P.O. Box 1034
Carmel Valley, CA 93924
phone: 408/659-2558
fax: 408/659-2588

This company is the developer of "The Datacom Agenda," a basic course in data communications with an emphasis on LANs and network integration. The course can be purchased by companies or departments and used to train managers, users, or any others who need a quick, thorough grounding in data communications.

Meta Group
19 Ludlow Road
Westport, CT 06880
phone: 203/226-6382
fax: 203/226-9009

New Science Associates, Inc.
167 Old Post Road
Southport, CT 06490
phone: 203/259-1661
fax: 203/254-1156

Probe Research, Inc.
Three Wing Drive
Cedar Knolls, NJ 07927-1097
phone: 201/285-1500
fax: 201/285-1519

Yankee Group
200 Portland Street
Boston, MA 02110
phone: 617/367-1000
fax: 617/367-5760

appendix E

E

Glossary
of LAN Terms

Access method   A set of rules that define how devices connected on a network gain access to the connecting medium to transmit information. (See Chapter 3.)

Asynchronous transmissions   Computer communications that occur one bit at a time, with start and stop bits at the beginning and end of each transmission. Typically simpler, less expensive, and slower than synchronous transmissions.

Backbone (or backbone network)   A common, high-speed medium, such as optical fiber, that links several LANs or computing resources. (See Chapter 2.)

Baseband cable   Cable that carries only one signal at a time. Baseband cable usually has a lower capacity than broadband cable.

BIOS   Basic input/output system, a basic component of a computer's operating system. Network operating systems must often enhance a BIOS to support multiple users or applications. NETBIOS is the standard set of enhancements for IBM PC-DOS and compatible operating systems. (See Chapter 3.)

Bit   A single small piece of electronic information. Computers process binary units (0 or 1); the word *bit* is derived from the phrase "binary digit."

Bridge   A combination of hardware and software used to link two or more LANs.

Broadband cable   Coaxial cable that can carry multiple signals along different channels simultaneously. Broadband cable can carry more information than baseband cable.

Bus   A path that can carry information signals. Also, a network topology in which connected devices are arranged in a continuous straight line. Many Ethernet LANs use the bus topology. (See Chapter 2.)

Byte   A small group of bits; typically eight bits.

CCITT   The Consultative Committee for International Telephony and Telegraphy, a worldwide standards body that works closely with other standards bodies, particularly the ISO. (See Chapter 9.)

Client-server computing Computing in an environment where individual systems, called servers, support multiple clients, or users' computers. Electronic mail is an example of a client-server application, in that part of the application runs on the server and part runs at the client workstation. LANs now are evolving into client-server networks. (See Chapters 5 and 9.)

Coaxial cable Cabling for information transmission that employs a single central conductor and two layers of insulation. Coaxial cable is used for a range of devices, from LANs to cable television. (See Chapter 2.)

Ethernet A LAN access method that allows connected devices to transmit randomly without any control over access to the connecting medium. If more than one device attempts to transmit data at the same time, both devices wait for different periods before attempting to retransmit data. (See Chapter 3.)

FDDI The Fiber Data Distributed Interface, an emerging standard for transmission of electronic information along fiber-optic cable. (See Chapter 9.)

Fiber-optic cable Network cabling that employs one or more optical fibers and carries information as light instead of electricity. Fiber-optic cable can carry more information farther than other types of LAN cabling, but it is expensive and may be difficult to install and maintain. (See Chapter 2.)

Gateway A combination of hardware and software that provides links between LANs, or from LANs to mainframes or minicomputers.

Hardware The actual chips, machines, and physical systems that contain and process software applications. (See Chapter 2.)

IEEE The Institute of Electrical and Electronic Engineers, a major developer and promoter of standards in the computing industry, including the 802 group of standards that defines network access methods such as Ethernet and Token Ring. (See Chapter 3.)

ISDN Integrated Services Digital Network, a set of recommended standards for rapid transmission of voice, data, and images over simple twisted-pair cables. ISDN-based facilities may become a popular method for linking LANs to each other and to other computers. (See Chapter 9.)

ISO   The International Standards Organization, the standards body responsible for the Open Systems Interconnect (OSI) model for network communication. The OSI model is being adopted as a standard for network communications around the world. (See Chapter 3.)

LAN   A combination of hardware and software that allows users' connected PCs, terminals, or workstations to share information and computing resources such as printers, storage space, software, and other computers. (See Chapter 1.)

Mainframe   A very large, powerful computing system. In the late 1960s and early 1970s, mainframes occupied entire rooms and required special air conditioning. Some still do. Desktop-to-mainframe links are a popular application for LANs.

MAN   A metropolitan-area network, or a network designed to span an area approximately the size of a small city. LAN-to-MAN connections are becoming increasingly important to many network managers and users. (See Chapter 1.)

Minicomputer   A computer that usually is larger and more powerful than a desktop PC, but smaller than a mainframe. Minicomputers are often used as departmental computers or large-scale servers for LANs.

Operating system   Basic computer software that allows computer systems to run applications. Network operating systems are often enhancements to operating systems designed for single computers. DOS and OS/2 are the most popular operating systems for IBM-compatible PCs. (See Chapter 3.)

Optical fiber   A fiber made of glass or plastic, typically the thickness of a human hair, that can carry electronic information as pulses of light. (See Chapter 2.)

PC   Short for personal computer. Although originally used almost exclusively to describe IBM-compatible systems, the term now applies to almost any desktop computer, whether a DOS or OS/2-based system or a Macintosh computer. (See Chapter 2.)

Protocol   A set of rules that govern specific actions, typically communication between computers. (See Chapter 3.)

Ring A network topology in which all connected devices are arranged in a ring shape, with no central hub. Ring networks are sometimes more difficult to expand than star- or bus-based networks. (See Chapter 2.)

Server A combination of hardware and software that provides particular services (such as communications or database access) to a number of connected users' computers. (See Chapter 2.)

SNA Systems Network Architecture, a set of rules developed by IBM that defines how computing networks are constructed. SNA is a proprietary standard, as opposed to OSI, which is an open standard. (See Chapter 3.)

Software The electronically encoded instructions that tell hardware what to do. (See Chapter 3.)

SQL The structured query language, a standard language for database access. SQL was developed by IBM for the mainframe world and is an evolving LAN standard. (See Chapter 9.)

Star A network topology in which connections to user workstations and other devices radiate from a central hub or server. (See Chapter 2.)

Synchronous transmissions Computer communications managed by a synchronizing clock. Bits are separated by fixed amounts of time. Synchronous transmissions typically are more complex, faster, and more expensive than asynchronous transmissions.

Terminal A desktop device that usually includes a screen and keyboard like a PC or workstation, but that requires connection to a computer to perform any important operations. Some terminals are similar to simple diskless workstations. (See Chapter 2.)

Token A bit of software that manages access to a network's connecting medium. Token-passing access methods (such as the Token Ring access method) avoid the conflicts possible when multiple devices try to communicate simultaneously (as with Ethernet). (See Chapter 3.)

Token Ring An access method that includes software that manages access to the connecting medium. A software token is passed around a ring-shaped network, and only the device that holds the token can transmit data. This access method was developed more recently than Ethernet and is endorsed by IBM. (See Chapter 3.)

Topology   The physical layout or arrangement of devices on a network. Popular LAN topologies include the bus, star, and ring topologies. (See Chapter 2.)

Twisted-pair cable   Cabling that employs pairs of copper wire twisted according to certain rules of physics to allow maximum information flow. Twisted-pair cables are found in LANs and most telephone systems. (See Chapter 2.)

Virus   Software designed to replicate itself and "infect" computing systems such as LANs. Viruses can be merely annoying or severely destructive to user information or network storage media. (See Chapter 5 and Appendix B.)

WAN   A wide-area network, or a network that can span one or several states or continents. LANs provide access to WANs for many corporate network users. (See Chapter 1.)

Workstation   Generally, a user's desktop computing system. Specifically, a diskless workstation is a PC-like terminal for LANs, usually without its own disk drives. An advanced workstation, in contrast, is a high-powered desktop computer, usually with more processing and storage facilities than most DOS-based or Macintosh PCs. (See Chapters 2 and 9.)

INDEX

3+Open network operating system (3Com), 89, 91
10-base-T standards, 148-149
802.x protocols, 39-40

A

access, protocols and standards for, 34–40
accountability and security, 51
advanced LANs
   vs. basic, 80–83, 108
   products for, 87–91
advanced workstations, 140–145
ALL-IN-1 e-mail service (Digital Equipment), 151
analyses and reliability, 168
ANSI (American National Standards Institute), 148
AppleTalk network, 18
application-specific integrated circuits, 126
ASCII files
   for backups, 68
   for file sharing, 37, 57
ASIC (application-specific integrated circuits), 126
ASP (Association of Shareware Publishers) seal on software, 74
assessment for choosing LANs, 97–101
AT&T cabling systems, 182–184
AUTOEXEC.BAT files, 84

B

Back-It programs (Gazelle Systems), 69, 71
BACKUP command (DOS), 69, 160–163
backup files, 160–163
   management of, 41
   and reliability, 67–72
   and virus protection, 167
bandwidth, 39
baseband cable, 186
basic ISDN rates, 146
basic LANs
   vs. advanced, 80–83, 108
   products for, 83–87
batch systems, 3
Bateson, Gregory, 154
broadband coaxial cable, 186
buffers, printer, 115–116
bulletin boards and viruses, 73–74
bus topologies, 26–27, 40, 108
buying LANs. *See* choosing LANs

C

cabling, 19–23, 174
   AT&T systems, 182–184
   for basic and advanced LANs, 82
   choosing, 106–107, 175–176, 186–187
   costs of, 185–187

IBM systems, 181–182
installation of, 179–180
placement of, 176–178
responsibility for, 178
standards for, 148–149
call-back modems, 51
central computers in star
topologies, 24
Certus LAN (FoundationWare), 52
chkdsk command (DOS), 161
choosing LANs, 7–8, 96–97
assessment of needs for, 97–101
basic vs. advanced, 80–91, 108
cabling for, 106–107, 175–176,
186–187
IBM vs. clones, 103–105
IBM vs. Macintosh, 105–106
and planning, 101–102
and strengths and weaknesses of
LANs, 119–121
topologies for, 107–108
classes, 155–156
client-server computing, 58–59,
132–133
clones, IBM, 13–14, 103–105
closed LANs, 35
CMIS (common management
information services) protocol,
150–151
CMOT (common management
over TCP/IP) protocol, 150–151
coaxial cable, 20–21, 175–176
for advanced LANs, 82
installation of, 180
vs. twisted-pair, 106–107
collisions, 25, 39
common management information
services protocol, 150–151
common management over TCP/IP
protocol, 150–151

Communications Server (Microsoft
and Digital Communications
Associates), 129–130
communications servers, 16–17,
128–130
compatibles, IBM, 13–14, 103–105
Computer Currents, 190
Concurrent DOS 386 multiuser
system (Digital Research), 118
Connect, 190–191
connections. *See* cabling
continuity of cabling, 180
conversion of files, 37, 57, 113
copies. *See* backup files
costs
for basic and advanced LANs,
82–83
for cabling, 185–187
and IBM clones, 103
PS/2, 134
CSMA/CD protocol, 39–40

D

Data Communications, 191
data disaster recovery planning,
66, 169
data switches for printers, 116–117
database servers, 17, 130–132
DataLens architecture (Lotus), 58
DataTrends Publications, Inc., 193
DB-Library (Microsoft), 131
DECconnect architecture (Digital
Equipment), 184–185
dedicated file servers, 16, 108
definitions of LANs, 2–7
DeskLink (Traveling Soft-
ware), 113
DeskMate user interface (Tandy),
152–153

desktop workstations, 15
DESQview (Quarterdeck), 136
deterministic network access
   methods, 38
disk servers, 3
diskless workstations, 14, 120
distributed system management, 170
documentation
   for cabling, 179
   creation of, 63–65
   personal, 59–60
   and reliability, 75–76
   site-specific, 62–63
   task-specific, 61–62
DOS, 32, 37, 133–137
dumb terminals, 12

E

Easy-PRINT systems (Tandy), 116
EISA group, 135
electrical interference. *See*
   interference
electronic mail, 132, 142, 151–152
electronic transmission standards,
   151–152
ELS LANs (Novell), 87
e-mail, 132, 142, 151–152
Ethernet protocols and standards,
   39, 107–108, 148–149
EtherSeries products (3Com), 87
expandability of LANs, 6
extended industry standard
   architecture, 135
extensions, operating system, 81

F

fault tolerance, 169

FDDI (fiber distributed data
   interface), 149
features, LAN, 5–7
fiber-optic cable, 21–22, 149
file servers, 3–4, 15–16
files
   conversion of, 37, 57, 113
   locking of, 34
   security for, 49–50
   sharing of, 112–114
   See also backup files
Finder program, 32
floppy disks, 12, 14
formatting of disks, 161–162
Forrester Research, 194
freeware and viruses, 73, 167
functional definition of LANs, 4–5

G

Gartner Group, Inc., 194
geographic scope of LANs, 6
graphical user interfaces, 152
grounding of cables, 179
group backups of files, 70–72
GUI (graphical user interface), 152

H

hard disk drives, 3, 12, 14–15, 114
hardware
   for basic and advanced
      LANs, 82
   listing of, 62, 75–76
   network interface adapters,
      17–19
   topologies, 7, 23–28, 107–108
   See also cabling; servers;
      workstations
heterogeneity of LANs, 7

history of LANs, 3–4
HP Network Services LAN
  Gateway (Hewlett-Packard), 129
HyperPAD (Brightbill-Roberts), 139

I

IBM systems
    cabling, 181–182
    vs. compatibles, 13–14, 103–105
    vs. Macintosh, 105–106, 139
industry standards. *See* standards
information sharing, 56–59
Information Systems Architecture, 182
Information Week, 191–192
integrated services digital network,
    145–147, 182–183
interactive systems, 3
interface standards, user, 152–153
interference
    in bus networks, 27
    and cabling, 179
    fiber-optic cable for, 21
International Data Corporation, 194
International Standards
    Organization, 36, 148
internet protocol, 150
Invisible Ethernet LAN (Invisible
    Software), 86
Invisible Network LAN (Invisible
    Software), 85–86
ISA (Information Systems
    Architecture), 182
ISDN (integrated services digital
    network), 145–147, 182–183
    primary rates for, 146–147
ISO (International Standards
    Organization), 36, 148

J

Jobs, Steven, 141

K

Kahn, Phillipe, 112
key disks for security, 50

L

LAN Manager (Microsoft)
    and Communications Server, 129
    and NetFrame servers, 126
    OS/2 support for, 134
LAN Times, 192
LANtastic LAN (Artisoft), 84–85
LapLink Mac (Traveling
    Software), 113
LapLink Plus (Traveling
    Software), 113
LocalTalk network, 18, 107
locking of files, 34
locks for security, 48
Lotus/DBMS server (Lotus), 132

M

Mach operating system, 142
Macintosh systems, 13–14,
    137–140
    AppleTalk for, 18
    vs. IBM, 105–106
    operating system for, 32
macros for backup files, 67–68, 70
magazines, 190–193
mainframe computers, 3
management, 7
    for security, 50–52

standards for, 150–151
tools for, 40–42, 170
MANs (metropolitan area
networks), 6
McDowell-Romero
Communications Consultants, 194
media. *See* cabling
memory, 13, 114
with Invisible Network, 85–86
for PCs and PS/2s, 134–135
mesh topology, 28
Meta group, 194
metropolitan area networks, 6
minicomputers, 3
MLS (Multi-LAN Switch) server
(Alantec), 129
modems, 17, 51
Motif interface (OSF), 144
Multi-LAN Switch server
(Alantec), 129
Multilink Advanced multiuser
system (Software Link), 119
multiple servers, 16
multitasking, DESQview for, 136
multiuser systems, 117–119
multivendor network standards, 150

N

National Institute for Standards
and Technology, 36
needs, assessment of, 97–101
NET program (LANtastic), 84
NET/30 operating system, 86
NETBIOS operating system, 81, 84
NetFrame servers, 125–127
NetWare LANs (Novell), 35,
88–89, 91
and 3+Open, 89
database server for, 131
and NetFrame servers, 126
software drivers for, 86

network interface adapters, 17–19
network operating systems, 32–34,
81–82, 84, 86, 89, 91
Network World, 192
New Science Associates, Inc., 195
newsletters, 193
NeXT systems, 141–143
NIC (network interface adapters),
17–19
NIST (National Institute for
Standards and Technology), 36
nodes
with bus networks, 27
in cost calculations, 83
nondedicated file servers, 16
number of users, 6

O

open LANs, 35
Open Look interface (AT&T), 144
open systems interconnect
network, 150
operating systems, network, 32–34,
81–82, 84, 86, 89, 91
optical fiber, 21–22, 149
Oracle Server (Oracle), 131–132
OS/2 operating system, 81–82
and clones, 104
database server for, 131
and DOS, 133–137
OSI (open systems interconnect)
network, 150

P

packets, 38–39
passwords, 48–49, 60
PC Magazine, 192
PC-PLUS multiuser system (Alloy
Computer), 118
PC-XBUS expansion unit (Alloy
Computer), 118

PCLAN/Server (Digital Equipment), 129
PCs (personal computers), 3, 12–15, 136
performance monitoring, 42
personal backup files, 67–70
personal computers, 3, 12–15, 136
personal documentation, 59–60
planning
    for data disaster recovery, 66, 169
    of LANs, 97, 100–102
    and reliability, 168
plenum cable, 177–178
point-to-point connections, 23
Portable NetWare LAN (Novell), 88–89
PostScript language (Adobe Systems), 153
power systems, backup, 41–42, 168–169
Premises Lightguide (AT&T), 183
Presentation Manager, 134
printers
    operating system control of, 34
    sharing of, 4, 15, 115–117
    standards for, 153
priority of access, 34
Probe Research, Inc., 195
problem resolution and reliability, 66, 74–75
PROFS e-mail service (IBM), 151
programs
    security for, 49–50
    sharing of, 112–114
protocols, 6, 35–40
PS/2s and PCs, 133–137

public-domain software and viruses, 73, 167

Q

Quattro spreadsheet (Borland), 136–137
queues, printer, 115

R

radial topology, 185
RAM (random-access memory), 13, 85
RAM boxes, 114
random network access methods, 38
recovery of data, 66, 169
redundancy, 6, 24, 169
reliability, 6, 65–66
    backup files for, 67–72
    and cabling, 19–20
    and documentation, 75–76
    and problem resolution, 74–75
    redundancy for, 6, 24, 169
    and resource management, 42
    service contracts for, 104
    systems approach to, 168–170
    and viruses, 72–74, 166–168
repeaters, signal, 25
research reports, 194
resellers, 83, 120
resources
    documentation of, 62, 75–76
    listing of, 62, 75–76
    management of, 42
    sharing of. *See* sharing

RESTORE command (DOS), 69,
  160–163
ring topologies, 24–26, 40
risk analysis, 169

S

SAA (Systems Applications
  Architecture), 37–38
SAMs (server-activated
  maintenance), 126
security, 7, 34, 46
  for files and programs, 49–50
  management-level concerns for,
    50–52
  for passwords, 48–49
  and reliability, 66
  for workstations and servers,
    47–48
selective backup copies, 69–70
seminars, 155–156
server-activated maintenance, 126
servers, 15–17
  for basic LANs, 82
  communications, 16–17,
    128–130
  database, 17, 130–132
  disk, 3
  evaluation of current, 124–125
  new, 125–127
  PCs as, 136
  printer, 4
  security for, 47–48
shadow RAM, 85
shareware and viruses, 73, 167
sharing
  of files, 4, 112–114
  of information, 56–59
  and multiuser systems, 117–119
  of printers, 4, 15, 115–117
shielded twisted-pair cables,
  19–20, 175–176

signal repeaters, 25
simple network management
  protocol, 150–151
site-specific documentation, 62–63
SNA (Systems Network
  Architecture), 37–38, 129–130
SneakerNet systems, 112–113
SNMP (simple network
  management protocol), 150–151
software
  for basic and advanced LANs,
    81–82
  documentation of, 75–76
  and viruses, 65–66, 72–74,
    166–168
SONET (synchronous optical
  network), 149
SPARCstations (Sun
  Microsystem), 141, 143
SQL Server (Microsoft), 131
SQLBase server (Gupta
  Technologies), 132
standards, 8, 36–40
  for cabling, 148–149
  EISA, 135
  management, 150–151
  printer, 153
  transmission, 148–149, 151–152
  user interface, 152–153
star topologies, 23–26
  cabling for, 181
  with DECconnect, 185
storage areas, sharing of, 113–114
StreetTalk naming service
  (VINES), 90
subdirectories, backing up of,
  162–163
SuperKey (Borland), 67
surface raceways for cabling,
  176–177
switch boxes, printer, 115–116

synchronous optical network, 149
system administration, 168
Systempro server (Compaq), 127
Systems Applications Architecture, 37–38
Systems Network Architecture, 37–38, 129–130
SYSTIMAX PDS (AT&T), 182–184

T

tape drive backups, 71–72
task-specific documentation, 61–62
TCP/IP protocol, 150
team backup of files, 70–72
technical definition of LANs, 4–5
telephone wiring, 20, 106–107
terminals, 3, 12–15
text-only files, 37
time-released viruses, 167
tokens and token-ring networks, 25, 39–40, 107–108
topologies, 7, 23–28, 107–108
TOPS LAN, 35, 87
traffic levels, monitoring of, 42
translation of files, 37, 57, 113
transmission control protocol, 150
transmission loss and cabling, 180
transmission standards, 148–149, 151–152
trends, 91–92
Trojan horse programs, 166
twisted-pair cables, 19–20, 175–176
    for AT&T systems, 183
    for basic LANs, 82
    vs. coaxial cables, 106–107
    installation of, 180
    standards for, 148–149
Type x cables, 182

U

UIO (Universal Information Outlet), 183
Unified Network Management Architecture (AT&T), 183
uninterruptible power supplies, 41, 66
Universal Information Outlet, 183
UNIX operating system, 143–145
    database server for, 131
    for VINES LAN, 90
UNMA (Unified Network Management Architecture) (AT&T), 183
UPS (uninterruptible power supplies), 41, 66
user groups, 155
users
    interface standards for, 152–153
    number of, 6
    and planning, 101–102
utilities, 33

V

vaccines for viruses, 72
VINES LAN (Banyan Systems), 90, 131
viruses, 65–66, 72–74, 166–168
volumes, 3
VROOMM technology (Borland), 137

W

WAN (wide area networks), 6
Windows (Microsoft), 134
wire closets, 179
wireless LANs, 22–23
wiring. *See* cabling
workstations, 12–15

advanced, 140–145
diskless, 14, 120
security for, 47–48
as servers, 82

X

X.25 protocol, 38

X.400 standard, 151
X.500 standard, 151–152
XCOPY command (DOS), 69
XTND architecture (Claris), 57–58

Y

Yankee Group, 195

Selections from The SYBEX Library

NETWORKS

The ABC's of Novell Netware
Jeff Woodward
282pp. Ref. 614-6

For users who are new to PC's or networks, this entry-level tutorial outlines each basic element and operation of Novell. The ABC's introduces computer hardware and software, DOS, network organization and security, and printing and communicating over the netware system.

Mastering Novell Netware
Cheryl C. Currid/Craig A. Gillett
500pp. Ref. 630-8

This book is a thorough guide for System Administrators to installing and operating a microcomputer network using Novell Netware. Mastering covers actually setting up a network from start to finish, design, administration, maintenance, and troubleshooting.

Networking with TOPS
Steven William Rimmer
350pp. Ref. 565-4

A hands on guide to the most popular user friendly network available. This book will walk a user through setting up the hardware and software of a variety of TOPS configurations, from simple two station networks through whole offices. It explains the realities of sharing files between PC compatibles and Macintoshes, of sharing printers and other peripherals and, most important, of the real world performance one can expect when the network is running.

OPERATING SYSTEMS

DOS User's Desktop Companion
SYBEX Ready Reference Series
Judd Robbins
969pp. Ref. 505-0

This comprehensive reference covers DOS commands, batch files, memory enhancements, printing, communications and more information on optimizing each user's DOS environment. Written with step-by-step instructions and plenty of examples, this volume covers all versions through 3.3.

Essential OS/2
(Second Edition)
Judd Robbins
445pp. Ref. 609-X

Written by an OS/2 expert, this is the guide to the powerful new resources of the OS/2 operating system standard edition 1.1 with presentation manager. Robbins introduces the standard edition, and details multitasking under OS/2, and the range of commands for installing, starting up, configuring, and running applications. For Version 1.1 Standard Edition.

Essential PC-DOS
(Second Edition)
Myril Clement Shaw
Susan Soltis Shaw
332pp. Ref. 413-5

An authoritative guide to PC-DOS, including version 3.2. Designed to make experts out of beginners, it explores everything from disk management to batch file programming. Includes an 85-page command summary. Through Version 3.2.

The ABC's of DOS 4
Alan R. Miller
275pp. Ref. 583-2

This step-by-step introduction to using DOS 4 is written especially for beginners. Filled with simple examples, *The ABC's of DOS 4* covers the basics of hardware, software, disks, the system editor EDLIN, DOS commands, and more.

ABC's of MS-DOS
(Second Edition)
Alan R. Miller
233pp. Ref. 493-3

This handy guide to MS-DOS is all many PC users need to manage their computer files, organize floppy and hard disks, use EDLIN, and keep their computers organized. Additional information is given about utilities like Sidekick, and there is a DOS command and program summary. The second edition is fully updated for Version 3.3.

DOS Instant Reference
SYBEX Prompter Series
Greg Harvey/Kay Yarborough Nelson
220pp. Ref. 477-1, 4 ¾" × 8"

A complete fingertip reference for fast, easy on-line help:command summaries, syntax, usage and error messages. Organized by function—system commands, file commands, disk management, directories, batch files, I/O, networking, programming, and more. Through Version 3.3.

Graphics Programming
Under Windows
Brian Myers/Chris Doner
646pp. Ref. 448-8

Straightforward discussion, abundant examples, and a concise reference guide to graphics commands make this book a must for Windows programmers. Topics range from how Windows works to programming for business, animation, CAD, and desktop publishing. For Version 2.

Hard Disk Instant Reference
SYBEX Prompter Series
Judd Robbins
256pp. Ref. 587-5, 4 ¾" × 8"

Compact yet comprehensive, this pocket-sized reference presents the essential information on DOS commands used in managing directories and files, and in optimizing disk configuration. Includes a survey of third-party utility capabilities. Through DOS 4.0.

Mastering DOS
(Second Edition)
Judd Robbins
722pp. Ref. 555-7

"The most useful DOS book." This seven-part, in-depth tutorial addresses the needs of users at all levels. Topics range from running applications, to managing files and directories, configuring the system, batch file programming, and techniques for system developers. Through Version 4.

The IBM PC-DOS Handbook
(Third Edition)
Richard Allen King
359pp. Ref. 512-3

A guide to the inner workings of PC-DOS 3.2, for intermediate to advanced users and programmers of the IBM PC series. Topics include disk, screen and port control, batch files, networks, compatibility, and more. Through Version 3.3.

MS-DOS Advanced
Programming
Michael J. Young
490pp. Ref. 578-6

Practical techniques for maximizing performance in MS-DOS software by making best use of system resources. Topics include functions, interrupts, devices, multitasking, memory residency and more, with examples in C and assembler. Through Version 3.3.

MS-DOS Handbook
(Third Edition)
Richard Allen King
362pp. Ref. 492-5

This classic has been fully expanded and revised to include the latest features of MS-DOS Version 3.3. Two reference books in one, this title has separate sections for programmer and user. Multi-DOS partitons, 3 ½-inch disk format, batch file call and return feature, and comprehensive coverage of MS-DOS commands are included. Through Version 3.3.

MS-DOS Power User's Guide, Volume I (Second Edition)
Jonathan Kamin
482pp. Ref. 473-9

A fully revised, expanded edition of our best-selling guide to high-performance DOS techniques and utilities—with details on Version 3.3. Configuration, I/O, directory structures, hard disks, RAM disks, batch file programming, the ANSI.SYS device driver, more. Through Version 3.3.

Programmers Guide to the OS/2 Presentation Manager
Michael J. Young
683pp. Ref. 569-7

This is the definitive tutorial guide to writing programs for the OS/2 Presentation Manager. Young starts with basic architecture, and explores every important feature including scroll bars, keyboard and mouse interface, menus and accelerators, dialogue boxes, clipboards, multitasking, and much more.

Programmer's Guide to Windows (Second Edition)
David Durant/Geta Carlson/Paul Yao
704pp. Ref. 496-8

The first edition of this programmer's guide was hailed as a classic. This new edition covers Windows 2 and Windows/386 in depth. Special emphasis is given to over fifty new routines to the Windows interface, and to preparation for OS/2 Presentation Manager compatibility.

Understanding DOS 3.3
Judd Robbins
678pp. Ref. 648-0

This best selling, in-depth tutorial addresses the needs of users at all levels with many examples and hands-on exercises. Robbins discusses the fundamentals of DOS, then covers manipulating files and directories, using the DOS editor, printing, communicating, and finishes with a full section on batch files.

Understanding Hard Disk Management on the PC
Jonathan Kamin
500pp. Ref. 561-1

This title is a key productivity tool for all hard disk users who want efficient, error-free file management and organization. Includes details on the best ways to conserve hard disk space when using several memory-guzzling programs. Through DOS 4.

Up & Running with Your Hard Disk
Klaus M Rubsam
140pp. Ref. 666-9

A far-sighted, compact introduction to hard disk installation and basic DOS use. Perfect for PC users who want the practical essentials in the shortest possible time. In 20 basic steps, learn to choose your hard disk, work with accessories, back up data, use DOS utilities to save time, and more.

UTILITIES

The ABC's of the IBM PC (Second Edition)
Joan Lasselle/Carol Ramsay
167pp. Ref. 370-8

Hands-on experience—without technical detail—for first-time users. Step-by-step tutorials show how to use essential commands, handle disks, use applications programs, and harness the PC's special capabilities.

Mastering the Norton Utilities
Peter Dyson
373pp. Ref. 575-1

In-depth descriptions of each Norton utility make this book invaluable for beginning and experienced users alike. Each utility is described clearly with examples and the text is organized so that readers can put Norton to work right away. Version 4.5.

Mastering PC Tools Deluxe
Peter Dyson
400pp. Ref. 654-5

A complete hands-on guide to the timesaving—and "lifesaving"—utility programs in Version 5.5 of PC Tools Deluxe. Contains concise tutorials and in-depth discussion of every aspect of using PC Tools—from high speed backups, to data recovery, to using Desktop applications.

Mastering SideKick Plus
Gene Weisskopf
394pp. Ref. 558-1

Employ all of Sidekick's powerful and expanded features with this hands-on guide to the popular utility. Features include comprehensive and detailed coverage of time management, note taking, outlining, auto dialing, DOS file management, math, and copy-and-paste functions.

Up & Running with Norton Utilities
Rainer Bartel
140pp. Ref. 659-6

Get up and running in the shortest possible time in just 20 lessons or "steps." Learn to restore disks and files, use UnErase, edit your floppy disks, retrieve lost data and more. Or use the book to evaluate the software before you purchase. Through Version 4.2.

COMMUNICATIONS

Mastering Crosstalk XVI (Second Edition)
Peter W. Gofton
225pp. Ref. 642-1

Introducing the communications program Crosstalk XVI for the IBM PC. As well as providing extensive examples of command and script files for programming Crosstalk, this book includes a detailed description of how to use the program's more advanced features, such as windows, talking to mini or mainframe, cus-

tomizing the keyboard and answering calls and background mode.

Mastering PROCOMM PLUS
Bob Campbell
400pp. Ref. 657-X

Learn all about communications and information retrieval as you master and use PROCOMM PLUS. Topics include choosing and using a modem; automatic dialing; using on-line services (featuring Compu-Serve) and more. Through Version 1.1b; also covers PROCOMM, the "shareware" version.

Mastering Serial Communications
Peter W. Gofton
289pp. Ref. 180-2

The software side of communications, with details on the IBM PC's serial programming, the XMODEM and Kermit protocols, non-ASCII data transfer, interrupt-level programming and more. Sample programs in C, assembly language and BASIC.

WORD PROCESSING

The ABC's of Microsoft Word (Third Edition)
Alan R. Neibauer
461pp. Ref. 604-9

This is for the novice WORD user who wants to begin producing documents in the shortest time possible. Each chapter has short, easy-to-follow lessons for both keyboard and mouse, including all the basic editing, formatting and printing functions. Version 5.0.

The ABC's of WordPerfect
Alan R. Neibauer
239pp. Ref. 425-9

This basic introduction to WordPefect consists of short, step-by-step lessons— for new users who want to get going fast. Topics range from simple editing and formatting, to merging, sorting, macros, and more. Includes version 4.2

The ABC's of WordPerfect 5
Alan R. Neibauer
283pp. Ref. 504-2
This introduction explains the basics of desktop publishing with WordPerfect 5: editing, layout, formatting, printing, sorting, merging, and more. Readers are shown how to use WordPerfect 5's new features to produce great-looking reports.

Advanced Techniques in Microsoft Word (Second Edition)
Alan R. Neibauer
462pp. Ref. 615-4
This highly acclaimed guide to WORD is an excellent tutorial for intermediate to advanced users. Topics include word processing fundamentals, desktop publishing with graphics, data management, and working in a multiuser environment. For Versions 4 and 5.

Advanced Techniques in MultiMate
Chris Gilbert
275pp. Ref. 412-7
A textbook on efficient use of MultiMate for business applications, in a series of self-contained lessons on such topics as multiple columns, high-speed merging, mailing-list printing and Key Procedures.

Advanced Techniques in WordPerfect 5
Kay Yarborough Nelson
586pp. Ref. 511-5
Now updated for Version 5, this invaluable guide to the advanced features of Word-Perfect provides step-by-step instructions and practical examples covering those specialized techniques which have most perplexed users—indexing, outlining, foreign-language typing, mathematical functions, and more.

The Complete Guide to MultiMate
Carol Holcomb Dreger
208pp. Ref. 229-9
This step-by-step tutorial is also an excellent reference guide to MultiMate features and uses. Topics include search/replace, library and merge functions, repagination, document defaults and more.

Introduction to WordStar
Arthur Naiman
208pp. Ref. 134-9
This all time bestseller is an engaging first-time introduction to word processing as well as a complete guide to using WordStar—from basic editing to blocks, global searches, formatting, dot commands, SpellStar and MailMerge. Through Version 3.3.

Mastering DisplayWrite 4
Michael E. McCarthy
447pp. Ref. 510-7
Total training, reference and support for users at all levels—in plain, non-technical language. Novices will be up and running in an hour's time; everyone will gain complete word-processing and document-management skills.

Mastering MultiMate Advantage II
Charles Ackerman
407pp. Ref. 482-8
This comprehensive tutorial covers all the capabilities of MultiMate, and highlights the differences between MultiMate Advantage II and previous versions—in pathway support, sorting, math, DOS access, using dBASE III, and more. With many practical examples, and a chapter on the On-File database.

Mastering Microsoft Word on the IBM PC (Fourth Edition)
Matthew Holtz
680pp. Ref. 597-2
This comprehensive, step-by-step guide details all the new desktop publishing developments in this versatile word processor, including details on editing, formatting, printing, and laser printing. Holtz uses sample business documents to demonstrate the use of different fonts, graphics, and complex documents. Includes Fast Track speed notes. For Versions 4 and 5.

Mastering WordPerfect
Susan Baake Kelly
435pp. Ref. 332-5
Step-by-step training from startup to mastery, featuring practical uses (form letters,

newsletters and more), plus advanced topics such as document security and macro creation, sorting and columnar math. Through Version 4.2.

Mastering WordPerfect 5
Susan Baake Kelly
709pp. Ref. 500-X
The revised and expanded version of this definitive guide is now on WordPerfect 5 and covers wordprocessing and basic desktop publishing. As more than 200,000 readers of the original edition can attest, no tutorial approaches it for clarity and depth of treatment. Sorting, line drawing, and laser printing included.

Mastering WordPerfect 5.1
Alan Simpson
1050pp. Ref. 670-7
The ultimate guide for the WordPerfect user. Alan Simpson, the "master communicator," puts you in charge of the latest features of 5.1: new dropdown menus and mouse capabilities, along with the desktop publishing, macro programming, and file conversion functions that have made WordPerfect the most popular word processing program on the market.

Mastering WordStar Release 5
Greg Harvey/David J. Clark
450pp. Ref. 491-7
This book is the ultimate reference book for the newest version of WordStar. Readers may use Mastering to look up any word processing function, including the new Version 5 and 5.5 features and enhancements, and find detailed instructions for fundamental to advanced operations.

Practical WordStar Uses
Julie Anne Arca
303pp. Ref. 107-1
A hands-on guide to WordStar and MailMerge applications, with solutions to comon problems and "recipes" for day-to-day tasks. Formatting, merge-printing and much more; plus a quick-reference command chart and notes on CP/M and PC-DOS. For Version 3.3.

Understanding WordStar 2000
David Kolodney/Thomas Blackadar
275pp. Ref. 554-9
This engaging, fast-paced series of tutorials covers everything from moving the cursor to print enhancements, format files, key glossaries, windows and MailMerge. With practical examples, and notes for former WordStar users.

Visual Guide to WordPerfect
Jeff Woodward
457pp. Ref. 591-3
This is a visual hands-on guide which is ideal for brand new users as the book shows each activity keystroke-by-keystroke. Clear illustrations of computer screen menus are included at every stage. Covers basic editing, formatting lines, paragraphs, and pages, using the block feature, footnotes, search and replace, and more. Through Version 5.

WordPerfect 5 Desktop Companion
SYBEX Ready Reference Series
Greg Harvey/Kay Yarborough Nelson
1006pp. Ref. 522-0
Desktop publishing features have been added to this compact encyclopedia. This title offers more detailed, cross-referenced entries on every software features including page formatting and layout, laser printing and word processing macros. New users of WordPerfect, and those new to Version 5 and desktop publishing will find this easy to use for on-the-job help.

WordPerfect 5 Instant Reference
SYBEX Prompter Series
Greg Harvey/Kay Yarborough Nelson
316pp. Ref. 535-2, 4 ¾" × 8"
This pocket-sized reference has all the program commands for the powerful WordPerfect 5 organized alphabetically for quick access. Each command entry has the exact key sequence, any reveal codes, a list of available options, and option-by-option discussions.

WordPerfect 5 Macro Handbook
Kay Yarborough Nelson
488pp. Ref. 483-6

Readers can create macros custom-tailored to their own needs with this excellent tutorial and reference. Nelson's expertise guides the WordPerfect 5 user through nested and chained macros, macro libraries, specialized macros, and much more.

WordPerfect Instant Reference
SYBEX Prompter Series
Greg Harvey/Kay Yarborough Nelson
254pp. Ref. 476-3, 4 3/4" × 8"

When you don't have time to go digging through the manuals, this fingertip guide offers clear, concise answers: command summaries, correct usage, and exact keystroke sequences for on-the-job tasks. Convenient organization reflects the structure of WordPerfect. Through Version 4.2.

WordPerfect Instant Reference
(2nd edition)
Greg Harvey/Kay Yarborough Nelson
316pp. Ref. 674-X

This pocket-sized reference has all the program commands for WordPerfect 5.0 and 5.1 organized alphabetically for quick reference. Each command has the exact key sequence, any reveal codes, a list of available options, and option-by-option discussions.

WordPerfect 5.1 Tips and Tricks
(Fourth Edition)
Alan R. Neibauer
675pp. Ref. 681-2

This new edition is a real timesaver. For on-the-job guidance and creative new uses, this title covers all versions of WordPerfect up to and including 5.1—streamlining documents, automating with macros, new print enhancements, and more.

WordStar Instant Reference
SYBEX Prompter Series
David J. Clark
314pp. Ref. 543-3, 4 3/4" × 8"

This quick reference provides reminders on the use of the editing, formatting, mailmerge, and document processing commands available through WordStar 4 and 5. Operations are organized alphabetically for easy access. The text includes a survey of the menu system and instructions for installing and customizing WordStar.

DATABASES

The ABC's of dBASE III PLUS
Robert Cowart
264pp. Ref. 379-1

The most efficient way to get beginners up and running with dBASE. Every 'how' and 'why' of database management is demonstrated through tutorials and practical dBASE III PLUS applications.

The ABC's of dBASE IV
Robert Cowart
338pp. Ref. 531-X

This superb tutorial introduces beginners to the concept of databases and practical dBASE IV applications featuring the new menu-driven interface, the new report writer, and Query by Example.

The ABC's of Paradox
Charles Siegel
300pp. Ref. 573-5

Easy to understand and use, this introduction is written so that the computer novice can create, edit, and manage complex Paradox databases. This primer is filled with examples of the Paradox 3.0 menu structure.

Advanced Techniques
in dBASE III PLUS
Alan Simpson
454pp. Ref. 369-4

A full course in database design and structured programming, with routines for inventory control, accounts receivable, system management, and integrated databases.

dBASE Instant Reference
SYBEX Prompter Series
Alan Simpson
471pp. Ref. 484-4; 4 3/4" × 8"

Comprehensive information at a glance: a

brief explanation of syntax and usage for every dBASE command, with step-by-step instructions and exact keystroke sequences. Commands are grouped by function in twenty precise categories.

dBASE IV Programmer's Instant Reference
SYBEX Prompter Series
Alan Simpson
544pp. Ref. 538-7, 4 ¾" × 8"
This comprehensive reference to every dBASE command and function has everything for the dBASE programmer in a compact, pocket-sized book. Fast and easy access to adding data, sorting, performing calculations, managing multiple databases, memory variables and arrays, windows and menus, networking, and much more. Version 1.1.

dBASE III PLUS Programmer's Reference Guide
SYBEX Ready Reference Series
Alan Simpson
1056pp. Ref. 508-5
Programmers will save untold hours and effort using this comprehensive, well-organized dBASE encyclopedia. Complete technical details on commands and functions, plus scores of often-needed algorithms.

dBASE IV User's Desktop Companion
SYBEX Ready Reference Series
Alan Simpson
950pp. Ref. 523-9
This easy-to-use reference provides an exhaustive resource guide to taking full advantage of the powerful non-programming features of the dBASE IV Control Center. This book discusses query by example, custom reports and data entry screens, macros, the application generator, and the dBASE command and programming language.

dBASE IV User's Instant Reference
SYBEX Prompter Series
Alan Simpson
349pp. Ref. 605-7, 4 ¾" × 8"
This handy pocket-sized reference book gives every new dBASE IV user fast and easy access to any dBASE command. Arranged alphabetically and by function, each entry includes a description, exact syntax, an example, and special tips from Alan Simpson.

Mastering dBASE III PLUS: A Structured Approach
Carl Townsend
342pp. Ref. 372-4
In-depth treatment of structured programming for custom dBASE solutions. An ideal study and reference guide for applications developers, new and experienced users with an interest in efficient programming.

Mastering dBASE IV Programming
Carl Townsend
496pp. Ref. 540-9
This task-oriented book introduces structured dBASE IV programming and commands by setting up a general ledger system, an invoice system, and a quotation management system. The author carefully explores the unique character of dBASE IV based on his in-depth understanding of the program.

Mastering Q & A (Second Edition)
Greg Harvey
540pp. Ref. 452-6
This hands-on tutorial explores the Q & A Write, File, and Report modules, and the Intelligent Assistant. English-language command processor, macro creation, interfacing with other software, and more, using practical business examples.

SYBEX Computer Books are different.

Here is why . . .

At SYBEX, each book is designed with you in mind. Every manuscript is carefully selected and supervised by our editors, who are themselves computer experts. We publish the best authors, whose technical expertise is matched by an ability to write clearly and to communicate effectively. Programs are thoroughly tested for accuracy by our technical staff. Our computerized production department goes to great lengths to make sure that each book is well-designed.

In the pursuit of timeliness, SYBEX has achieved many publishing firsts. SYBEX was among the first to integrate personal computers used by authors and staff into the publishing process. SYBEX was the first to publish books on the CP/M operating system, microprocessor interfacing techniques, word processing, and many more topics.

Expertise in computers and dedication to the highest quality product have made SYBEX a world leader in computer book publishing. Translated into fourteen languages, SYBEX books have helped millions of people around the world to get the most from their computers. We hope we have helped you, too.

For a complete catalog of our publications:

SYBEX, Inc. 2021 Challenger Drive, #100, Alameda, CA 94501
Tel: (415) 523-8233/(800) 227-2346   Telex: 336311
Fax: (415) 523-2373

TO JOIN THE SYBEX MAILING LIST OR ORDER BOOKS
PLEASE COMPLETE THIS FORM

NAME _____ COMPANY _____

STREET _____ CITY _____

STATE _____ ZIP _____

☐ PLEASE MAIL ME MORE INFORMATION ABOUT **SYBEX** TITLES

ORDER FORM (There is no obligation to order)

PLEASE SEND ME THE FOLLOWING:

TITLE	QTY	PRICE
_____	____	____
_____	____	____
_____	____	____
_____	____	____

TOTAL BOOK ORDER _____ $_____

CUSTOMER SIGNATURE _____

SHIPPING AND HANDLING PLEASE ADD $2.00 PER BOOK VIA UPS _____

FOR OVERSEAS SURFACE ADD $5.25 PER BOOK PLUS $4.40 REGISTRATION FEE _____

FOR OVERSEAS AIRMAIL ADD $18.25 PER BOOK PLUS $4.40 REGISTRATION FEE _____

CALIFORNIA RESIDENTS PLEASE ADD APPLICABLE SALES TAX _____

TOTAL AMOUNT PAYABLE _____

☐ CHECK ENCLOSED ☐ VISA
☐ MASTERCARD ☐ AMERICAN EXPRESS

ACCOUNT NUMBER _____

EXPIR. DATE _____ DAYTIME PHONE _____

CHECK AREA OF COMPUTER INTEREST:

☐ BUSINESS SOFTWARE

☐ TECHNICAL PROGRAMMING

☐ OTHER: _____

THE FACTOR THAT WAS MOST IMPORTANT IN YOUR SELECTION:

☐ THE SYBEX NAME

☐ QUALITY

☐ PRICE

☐ EXTRA FEATURES

☐ COMPREHENSIVENESS

☐ CLEAR WRITING

☐ OTHER _____

OTHER COMPUTER TITLES YOU WOULD LIKE TO SEE IN PRINT:

_____

_____

OCCUPATION

☐ PROGRAMMER ☐ TEACHER

☐ SENIOR EXECUTIVE ☐ HOMEMAKER

☐ COMPUTER CONSULTANT ☐ RETIRED

☐ SUPERVISOR ☐ STUDENT

☐ MIDDLE MANAGEMENT ☐ OTHER:

☐ ENGINEER/TECHNICAL _____

☐ CLERICAL/SERVICE

☐ BUSINESS OWNER/SELF EMPLOYED

CHECK YOUR LEVEL OF COMPUTER USE

☐ NEW TO COMPUTERS

☐ INFREQUENT COMPUTER USER

☐ FREQUENT USER OF ONE SOFTWARE

  PACKAGE:

  NAME _____

☐ FREQUENT USER OF MANY SOFTWARE

  PACKAGES

☐ PROFESSIONAL PROGRAMMER

OTHER COMMENTS:

_____

_____

_____

_____

_____

_____

_____

PLEASE FOLD, SEAL, AND MAIL TO SYBEX

SYBEX, INC.
2021 CHALLENGER DR. #100
ALAMEDA, CALIFORNIA USA
          94501

SEAL